3

Contemporary Landscapes
in Mixed Media

Contemporary Landscapes
in Mixed Media

Soraya French

BATSFORD

This book is dedicated to my amazing family, Tim, Yasmin and Saasha, for their unconditional love and for gracefully embracing the chaotic experience of living with a working artist.

Page 1
September Fields
35.5 x 35.5 cm (14 x 14 in)

Page 2
Distant Poppy Field
47 x 40.5 cm (18 ½ x 16 in)

Page 3
Willowherb Field
30.5 x 30.5 cm (12 x 12 in)

First published in the United Kingdom in 2017 by
Batsford
43 Great Ormond Street
London WC1N 5HZ

An imprint of Pavilion Books Company Ltd

ISBN 978-1-84994-356-7

A CIP catalogue record for this book is available from the British Library.

10 9 8 7 6 5 4 3 2 1

Reproduction by Mission Productions Ltd, Hong Kong
Printed and bound by 1010 Printing International Ltd, China
This book can be ordered direct from the publisher at www.pavilionbooks.com.

Contents

Introduction

The broad and multi-dimensional world of making art in mixed media has many wonderful surprises in store to be explored. This form of painting can even be described as the ultimate creative indulgence, where you can take delight in the seductive qualities of transparent media such as inks and watercolours as well as enjoying the versatility and forgiving nature of the opaque media such as acrylics and pastels. It gives you the chance to use many other mark-making materials too, both traditional and innovative; the infinite combinations offer you tremendous freedom and flexibility to interpret your favourite subjects in unique ways that burst with life and energy.

◁ **The Scottish Landscape**
46 x 56 cm (18 x 22 in)

The aim of this book

I hope that the passion and enthusiasm that has gone into producing this book will in turn inspire those of you ready to take the plunge into the wonderland that is painting in mixed media. Be prepared to open your mind and think beyond the limited boundaries of expressing your ideas in a single medium and the inevitable rules and limitations that go with the territory. The wealth of art materials available and the freedom of expression allowed today create a potent combination for imaginative artists who wish to expand their creative potential and think outside the box of the more traditional disciplines.

Don't feel overwhelmed by the amount of information and the array of art materials within these pages – you don't need them all. Instead, treat the book as a source of reference to try out new ways of using the materials as and when you come across them in your artistic adventures. Equipping yourself with more art materials certainly doesn't equate to being a better painter – in fact it can be rather confusing. The amount of information is to help you make thoughtful choices, not to encourage you to acquire every type of medium available to man. Take what is relevant and appealing to you and leave the rest. Unless otherwise stated, the acrylic paints and products used in this book are from Golden Artist Colors and the pastels are from Sennelier, but you will find most named colours available from other brands. The watercolour paper is Saunders Waterford from St Cuthbert's Mill.

Mixed media work is often characterized by multiple layers, which give the paintings their rich and interesting visual appeal. You can use the media in an incredibly complex and elaborate manner or go for a simpler, understated approach. Whatever you choose, however, make it your own. Be inventive and explore interpretations unique to yourself. Many of the techniques we enjoy today are the legacies left by the visionary past masters. However, each generation of artists revamps existing ideas to make them fresh and relevant to the present era.

In this book you will find:

• Comprehensive information regarding the materials and some of the possible techniques on their own or in combination with one another.

• Projects to inspire you to try out exercises that will help you to further your knowledge of mixed media.

• Demonstrations to guide you through the stages of painting, either a complex scene or an ordinary subject made more interesting through texture.

• Something of every level of ability for anyone who is ready to take a creative leap forward. The only limit is how far you are prepared to explore.

▷ **Violet Sky**
38 x 38 cm (15 x 15 in)

A personal note

This book is a collection of old and new paintings, plus a series of one-off exercises simply to show a particular technique. As a great believer in artistic growth through experimentation I try not to get too comfortable in any one period of my painting journey, however successful. Getting older has its compensations, too; I am more patient and have learnt to accept what I can or can't achieve and try to enjoy the process regardless of the end result. This breakthrough certainly keeps disappointment at bay and has helped me to survive the inevitable struggles and triumphs that every working artist goes through. I have become increasingly brave at taking risks and am not daunted by the possible failures in order to achieve exciting results and get away from the safe and boring.

My 'eureka' moment in this journey came about accidentally by discovering that painting on a pristine white support and the need for planning ahead had a negative effect on my creativity. Fortunately, by this time I had used each medium on its own for a number of years and I was ready to step into the magical and liberating world of painting in mixed media. This meant that I could indulge in my passion for transparent media as well as enjoying the more controlled and texturizing effects of the opaque materials. I became more spontaneous and felt free from the confines of working in a single medium.

The organic process of painting on a chaotic surface that is marked without being intended for a specific subject matter is truly a fulfilling experience. Manipulating and consolidating the abstract shapes and bringing some kind of order to the chaos is the process I enjoy most. I let the painting evolve naturally and keep an open mind, as I find that too much focus on the end result can be counterproductive and a waste of creative energy.

△ **Autumn Hedgerow**
51 x 25.5 cm (20 x 10 in)

I am obsessed with pigment and unashamedly confess to being a total colour nerd, but when it comes to my painting, I try to use it intuitively and not let colour theory get in the way of my emotional involvement with the subject. The colourful and painterly style of the Impressionists' paintings mesmerized me as a young student and the artists of the Nabis and the Fauvist movements in particular had a great influence in opening my eyes to the wonderful world of colour. I love and admire artists who use colour in a big-hearted and unselfconscious way. Painting the emotional energy rather than the physical reality of what is in front of me is more important to me than the subject matter. For that reason you won't find specific landmarks or places in my landscapes. My paintings are simply a result of my heartfelt response to the subject through many layers of colour, texture and pattern and I hope that I can transfer the same joyful experience to the viewer.

▷ Summer
Hedgerow
53.5 x 51 cm
(21 x 20 in)

Discovering your unique artistic voice

In every genre of art, originality and authenticity are two very important ingredients that set you apart from the crowd. It is important to be identified as an individual artist and not a paler copy of artists you admire. Fortunately, with regular practice and dedication, your individuality will shine through. Along the way you may emulate artists who inspire you in order to hone your necessary skills of expression, but there comes a time when this practice becomes rather pointless and unsatisfactory and you feel ready to develop your own unique visual language to communicate with your audience. Using your intuition and listening to your most honest inner voice, together with some risk-taking, should help you take a creative leap towards discovering your own unique and resonant voice. However, it is important not to get too secure and comfortable in the style you have found, which can lead to creating stagnant and repetitive art work. To avoid this trap, it is advisable to step out of your comfort zone from time to time and energize your work through experimenting with new ideas. Painting in mixed media should help you tremendously by offering the infinite ways of combining mediums and techniques. The forgiving nature of mixed media and the lack of too many rules should help you become more spontaneous and adopt a more carefree attitude, which is the perfect combination for healthy artistic growth.

Materials and techniques

Mixed media encompasses a broad range of materials and techniques, and the sheer variety available today can make deciding what to use a daunting task. In this chapter I shall guide you through the maze of different media, explaining their properties and unique characteristics, plus some of the many possible combinations of them. The interplay of different media is the most stimulating and exciting part of painting in this way. There are no hard and fast rules to limit your creativity, except that technical compatibility should be taken into consideration to ensure the success and ultimately the longevity of your artworks.

◁ **Daisies on Clifftop**
46 x 63.5 cm (18 x 25 in)

Acrylics – the wonder medium

Acrylics come in different levels of viscosity, so the artist can choose whether to employ oil painting techniques with the thicker consistency or use the more liquid forms of fluid acrylics and inks for watercolour techniques – or even combine all viscosities. Indeed acrylic can be described as jack and master of all trades.

This versatility makes acrylics the ideal choice as the main player in a mixed media painting. By nature acrylics dry within a short space of time to allow for many glazes or textural layers to follow. They combine beautifully with other mediums such as all types of pastels; they can make a base for oil colours, combine with collage beautifully and even act as glue.

Acrylics can be used on most surfaces apart from a shiny or greasy support. You can apply thick paint right from the start and glaze with thinner layers without the fear of cracking, or you can start with thinner paint and move on to thicker. This freedom will help you get to grips with acrylics more quickly than with media that come with a set of specific rules.

Gloss or matte mediums can change the sheen and appearance of your acrylics and extend the paint. Pour the required amount in a small container to dip into and mix with your paint. By adding more medium your colours can become quite translucent. When using mediums with your paints, water becomes just the means to wash your brushes in between paint applications.

Most paint manufacturers provide an economical range, known as student grade, and a far superior variety described as artist quality. The latter are slightly more expensive but they have a higher proportion of top quality pigments, which means the paint goes further, while not compromising the quality of your art. Golden Artist Colors advise artists to mix artist quality colours with one of the gels to make them stretch further. Investing in the best artist quality colours, gauging the right amount of water and making expressive brush marks bring out the best in this amazing and versatile medium.

◁ **The Edge of the Cornfield**
28 x 40.5 cm (11 x 16 in)
This painting is a good example of how you can use heavy body acrylics quite thickly in an impasto style (the foreground) and then slightly dilute them for another passage (the trees) in the same painting.

▷ **Trees on the Hillside**
40.5 x 40.5 cm (16 x 16 in)

No brushes were used in the creation of this painting. For most parts I used old credit cards to scrape the heavy body acrylic paint on, as well as a roller in the foreground. I also manipulated the paint with my finger in places. I cut up some of the cards into small pieces to paint the skeletal trees and branches. Marks made in this way are far less contrived than brushwork and can be quite interesting. I love the hit and miss nature of applying paint like this, allowing tiny glimpses of the underpainting colour to poke through the layers.

Beyond brushes

A thin and transparent medium such as watercolour requires good-quality brushes to perform at its best. When painting with acrylic you can go beyond brushes and not only have fun with the paint but create some wonderful textures in the process. Try scraping the paint on with a card, rolling it on, applying it with your fingers or a palette knife, scratching into thick paint with a sharp object or using various items to print an impression on the paint surface. There are also plenty of gadgets available, such as colour shapers and the Catalyst range of blades and wedges with a silicon head in a variety of shapes, to help you make interesting marks and textures. Of course, we all have our collection of favourite brushes as well, with watercolour brushes for inks and stiffer brushes for heavy body acrylics. Ultimately, be inventive with your mark-making and step outside the norm to be rewarded by a more interesting surface quality to your paintings.

Acrylic inks

I find splashes of vibrant acrylic inks by far the most unpredictable and exciting means of applying colour to paper or canvas. Inks are the most fluid form of acrylic colours and can be used with all types of watercolour techniques. They make the most mesmerizing shapes in wet-into-wet applications to create atmospheric backgrounds, while a combination of wet washes on dry paper and wet-into-wet application can create wonderful patterns of hard and soft edges.

One of the great advantages of acrylic inks over watercolour is the fact that a dry layer of colour cannot be disturbed by a subsequent wet wash. This helps the colours to retain their freshness and vibrancy. Marker pens with a variety of nibs can be filled with the inks to give you a greater degree of control for finer details or broad strokes of colour with larger nibs. The viscosity of the heavy body acrylics can result in quite clumsy marks when you need very fine lines in your painting, while the fluidity of inks helps you to create these with ease using a rigger brush or a marker with a really fine nib. For even background colour, you can apply the inks with a spray bottle or use an airbrush.

Inks also play a large part in mixed media paintings for their glorious interaction with paper collage which creates the most wonderful and random shapes. After 25 years, I still find acrylic inks just as exciting and beautiful to work with as I did when I first used them.

◁ **Teasels**
40.5 x 51 cm
(16 x 20 in)
This study of teasels was done with splashes of Sepia, Hansa Yellow Medium, Process Magenta and Process Cyan, allowing the inks to mingle and create a series of beautifully random hard and soft edges.

△ **Seashore Fireworks**
54.5 x 61 cm (21½ x 24 in)

Fluid colours have a heavier viscosity than inks, so you can successfully flick lovely strands of colour over the support. In this painting I diluted Fluid Phthalo Blue to apply the base wash across the sky and the sea, then flicked long strands of yellow, orange, green and blue Fluid colours across the paper to create this tangled mass in the foreground.

Fluid acrylics

Artist quality Fluid acrylics have a consistency similar to double cream, thicker than ink and runnier than the heavy body colours but with the same amount of water and pigment load. They are highly intense and permanent. You cannot produce Fluid acrylics by adding water to your heavy body colours – this will only give a rather weaker and much lighter version of your heavy body paint with thinner film and less adhesive quality – nor should you use the thin and runny student grade colours rather than the artist quality range.

Both inks and Fluid paints are ideal for spraying, brushing, staining, splattering and all manner of random mark-making. The Fluid colours are particularly good for pouring techniques as well as flicking long strands of colour across the support in Jackson Pollock style, an effective way of creating a random and pleasing mark. The inks are too thin and the heavy body colours are too thick for this purpose.

Heavy body paints can be rather clumsy where you need finer lines, and this is where you can use either inks or Fluids successfully with markers, a ruling pen or a rigger brush.

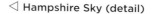

◁ **French Furrowed Fields**
40.5 x 38 cm (16 x 15 in)

Open acrylics are ideal for sgraffito technique, where a layer of colour is applied as underpainting and the subsequent layer is scratched into, revealing the underpainting. Open colours stay wet long enough to allow you to build up your layers before you make your sgraffito marks. In this painting I used Flame Orange ink to create a warm underpainting and then painted the top layers with Open acrylics. This way I had plenty of time to paint, knowing that I could still make my sgraffito marks to suggest the furrows in the field.

Acrylics with an extended open time

If you love pushing the paint around the canvas or paper for long periods of time, you can opt for acrylics with an extended open time. Golden Open acrylics stay wet long enough for blending techniques, all types of oil and acrylic painting and several printmaking techniques that require a longer working time. Their longer workable life on your palette also cuts down waste considerably. Unlike oils, Open acrylics can be dried using a hairdryer to speed up the application of a subsequent layer of paint.

Golden Open have their own gels and mediums to help keep the same extended open time, since gels and mediums from the standard fast-drying acrylics would cut down the drying time of these paints. They can also be mixed with standard fast-drying acrylics as well as all the gels and pastes on pp.56–69, but their longer drying time will be reduced according to the ratio of the mixture. This means that if you want to slightly speed up the drying time of Open colours you can mix them with some fast-drying acrylics and vice versa.

If you intend to use both Open and fast-drying acrylics separately in one painting, it is best to use the fast-drying colour in the first few layers to avoid cracking of the surface. Alternatively, use the fast-drying colours over perfectly dry Open colours.

Open acrylics work just as well with other media and collage and can be a useful addition to a mixed media art box. They are the ideal form of acrylics for painting en plein air, especially in hotter climates.

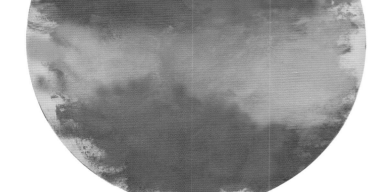

◁ **Hampshire Sky (detail)**

The extended working time of Open acrylics is perfect for blending techniques such as softening the edges of cloud formations. In this small sky study I applied a number of colours, safe in the knowledge that I had plenty of time to move around the colours and render the contours diffuse.

Watercolours

There is no denying the beauty and seductive qualities of watercolours. For the most part, acrylic inks tend to replace them in mixed media but there are times when I may need to lift colour or I feel that glazing an area with watercolour would be beneficial. More importantly, there may be a certain colour that I favour in my watercolour range. There are also particular textural effects to be gained, such as the interaction of watercolours with salt or granulating medium that is unique to this beautiful and popular medium; using clingfilm to create crease-like textures works best with them too. You will probably find that using watercolours as part of a mixed media painting rather than on their own helps you to relax and handle the paints in a more free and uninhibited manner, giving the appearance of more energy and vitality.

Gouache

Gouache is really watercolour but with some added body to give you the option of layering lighter opaque colours over the darker values. You can also use gouache by diluting it to give it the transparency of watercolour. I have a special fondness for gouache as it was my choice of medium during my teenage years. I love its opacity and matte surface and where I feel these characteristics can contribute to my painting I turn to it.

A very effective way of using gouache is to layer a few colours and let them dry, then rewet the surface selectively and lift colour to create some wonderful abstract shapes. Today you can also buy acrylic gouache with a matte finish in some wonderful pastel shades that can be very effective where you need these softer colours and a very matte surface.

◁ **Hogweed**
I painted the background here using lovely vibrant Phthalo Blue, Quinacridone Magenta and Green Gold. I then used Titanium White gouache to paint the flower head. The opacity of gouache also meant that I could bring my lighter green stems of the hogweed over the dried watercolour passages, using a rigger brush.

Pastels

Dry drawing media such as different varieties of pastels allow you to paint and draw simultaneously. I love the way this type of mark-making tool removes the barriers between the artist and the artwork; you are holding the pigment in your hand and are much closer to the painting surface. The direct contact often releases a different type of creative energy that results in more expressive marks.

Soft pastel

This is a direct, immediate and responsive medium. As a dry and highly permanent medium it has no shift in tone; the colour retains its vibrancy without becoming lighter or darker. The vivid colours of the brighter hues of pastel can transform a mixed media painting and add a touch of magic. Pastels should ideally be applied to a surface that has enough tooth to grip the powder. In mixed media painting acrylic paint and gouache can both create a certain amount of tooth, but there are also acrylic-based primers, such as Golden Acrylic Ground for Pastels, that can transform a smooth card into a suitable surface for pastel used alone or in mixed media. Alternatively, you can choose a type of wet and dry artist quality sandpaper that already has enough tooth.

Artist quality soft pastels are almost like pure pigment with just enough binder and very little filler and extender. They are often round in shape and are a joy to work with. The slightly harder pastels are usually square and can be pressed harder if you need to make a mark with more emphasis. By incorporating soft pastels into my mixed media work, I get my pastel 'fix' without having to use them extensively and breathe in a lot of dust. Dry mediums can add accents of brilliant colour in a way that is harder or even impossible to achieve with wet media.

◁ This is a detail of a larger painting showing how I applied long and narrow strokes of Naples Yellow and Yellow Ochre soft pastels over acrylics to describe the strands of wheat in the field.

▽ Derelict Barns

48.5 x 63.5 cm (19 x 25 in)

Pastel is such a responsive and direct medium. This painting was done on artist quality sandpaper, which takes quite a number of layers before it becomes saturated. I made rather definite marks and left them without blending, which creates a much livelier surface than over blended pastels. This helps the jewel-like colours retain their brilliance and vibrancy.

Oil pastel

The vibrancy and rich texture of artist quality oil pastels can enhance a mixed media painting beautifully. You can apply the pastels at the early stages to resist the washes of colour or as accents or highlights over acrylics, gouache or watercolour. Should you need to eliminate the oil pastel marks you can cover the unwanted areas with heavy body acrylic paint as the pastels do not contain active oils and their tacky surface is quite receptive, but they will always act as a resist under washes of watercolour or ink. If you need to make a wash of colour with oil pastels, use a little thinner with a rag or a brush to move the colours around. Artist quality oil pastels vary from one brand to another in softness and the range of colours, so experiment with a few to find the right one for your needs.

▽ **Seaweed and Waves**
35.5 x 38 cm (14 x 15 in)

Scribbles of bright yellow and vivid lime green plus black created areas of resist under washes of Phthalo Blue High Flow (acrylic inks) and Golden Fluid Manganese Blue Light and Titanium White. I love seeing the nuances of oil pastel peeping through the ink washes. It makes for a much more spontaneous look than if the weeds were painted with intention.

Crayons and pencils

Artist quality wax crayons make another useful addition to the mixed media collection. Pure wax crayons can be used in dry form to enhance and highlight; they resist washes of colour in a similar way to oil pastels but have a much harder consistency. Water-soluble wax crayons can also be useful, either as a dry mark or mixed with water to create colour washes and thin glazes.

Coloured pencils can bring linear marks and fine lines when needed, while watercolour pencils and water-soluble crayons are the perfect media for minimal outlines at the beginning of the painting as they can then merge into the rest of the colours. These are great for sketching outdoors, using water, a brush and a small sketch pad.

Spray paints

While spray paints were once mainly associated with urban and graffiti artists, they have gradually found their way into the mainstream art world. I use Montana Gold sprays for applying a soft all-over colour to banish the white ground of the canvas or paper, especially for large works when I require an even colour application. I also find them the perfect tool for applying colour with stencils in a variety of different shapes. There are a whole range of beautiful metallic, transparent and the more opaque Shock colours to choose from.

As well as the colours that are available, Montana Effect sprays add a whole new dimension to the creative process with spray cans. These will enable you to create some unusual and highly effective textures such as Granit, Crackle and my favourite, Marble Effect. It takes a little patience and practice to get to grips with the coordination required to use two spray cans simultaneously for seamless applications and blending of colours but it is worth the time and effort to master this. It is best to use the spray cans outside or in an extremely well ventilated room, preferably wearing a mask for the fumes and goggles to protect your eyes.

△ **Golden Sand**
35.5 x 56 cm (14 x 22 in)
For this painting I applied a thin layer of texture to create a slightly raised effect over the sea, then sprayed it with blue Shock colour and scratched some horizontal lines into the surface before the paint dried.
I applied turquoise spray on the seashore for the shallow waters. Heavy sprays of light grey Granit Effect provided the right texture to suggest the roughness of the pebbles on the beach. I then used yellow, yellow ochre and orange in varying degrees to paint the beach. The white marble-effect spray seemed to be the perfect tool to provide the spray of the waves.

▽ **Fishing Nets**

45 x 45 cm (18 x 18 in)

I started this painting by spraying Montana Transparent yellow in the sky area, then masking the sun with a round lid. I applied further Transparent colours, purple, blue and yellow. I then used Montana Texture to create a little texture on the cottages. Grey Granit Effect provided the perfect texture for the harbour wall. Fruit netting, a few smaller round lids for the fenders and some framing cord were placed as stencils to suggest the ropes. I applied layers of blue and red (Shock colours) and purple and yellow (Transparent colours) in varying degrees to mask out the stencils. When the paint dried, I lifted the stencils gently to reveal the shapes. I sprayed the cottage walls with white, then mixed red and yellow on my palette and applied it on the rooftops and the fenders.

Combining different media

There are no hard and fast rules about combining different media, though getting to know the particular characteristics unique to each one makes the painting process more enjoyable. Familiarize yourself with each medium through play sessions without the pressure of trying to produce a masterpiece. To begin with, carry out uncomplicated exercises that involve just two mediums. This way you will get to know how they interact before starting a more complex project.

Oil pastels can help you create a resist effect if you use them under a wash of colour from any water-based media that can be applied in diluted form; you can apply oil paints over an acrylic base but not the other way round, due to the much longer drying process of oils as well as the fact that the acrylic may peel off at a later stage. A dry medium such as soft pastel should be applied over dry patches of water media as the colour would be lost under a wet wash, so use it at the latter stages of your painting. Compatibility of media is paramount, not only in the process of mixing them together but also in order to avoid compromising the longevity of the painting.

The number of media and techniques gives you endless opportunities for experimentation. Failed paintings or exercises are brilliant teachers, so don't throw them away. Keep them as reminders of what went wrong, rework the unwanted areas or prime the paper with gesso for a fresh piece of work.

◁ **Colourful Rocks (detail)**
Here washes of High Flow acrylics create wonderful patterns over the tissue paper collage I used for the texture of the rocks. These highly pigmented and lightfast inks help to reinforce the colours of tissue paper, which is prone to fading. The colours of the rocks were further enhanced and highlighted by accents of soft pastel over the dried tissue collage. The fields in the background have a dusting of Bright Turquoise soft pastel to contrast with and cool the warmer olive green.

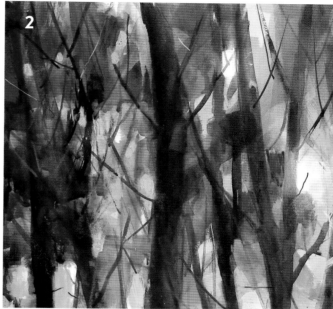

1. A prepared ground with texture paste, heavy body acrylics and oil pastel as accents of colour.
2. Wax crayons over washes of ink to enhance their colours, plus oil pastel used as a resist.
3. Royal blue soft pastel applied over dark blue acrylic to enhance the colour.
4. Acrylic ink over sculpted extra heavy gel enhanced with colourful wax crayons.

Project 1: Mark-making

Every painting is just a collection of marks; it is the quality of these marks that determines the success of the work. As young children, long before we learn to write we engage easily and spontaneously in the joyful sensation of mark-making with whatever tool comes to hand, whether it be pencil, chalk, crayon or even food items such as chocolate. Unfortunately, this natural and uninhibited ability diminishes as we become adults and strive for perfection.

So this exercise challenges you to find the child within yourself and set aside the urge to create a recognizable image – just use the collection of materials in an intuitive and creative way personal to you to practise and improve your mark-making ability. Take advantage of the tactile nature of your drawing media to really engage with your chosen support, which could be canvas or any type of paper. Use unconventional tools, cards, rollers or fingers without the pressure of producing a finished image – you should feel liberated to engage with your materials directly, getting to know them intimately and to discover how far you can push the boundaries of each one. Combine wet and dry media and change the sequence of application of one over the other to explore the difference. This project should help you find ways of creating random marks that make the painting process look effortless and spontaneous.

△ **Intuitive mark-making concertina sketch book**
Making marks without any specific image in mind is a great exercise that can free up your painting style. This is my section of a very long mark-making exercise done by 35 artists and made into a small concertina book for each artist. I also buy ready-made concertina sketch pads to make small mark-making samples to use in larger pieces of work.

1. Acrylic markers are great for drawing into washes to create either random or recognizable shapes.

2. Scraping the paint on a surface textured with gesso and some collage creates a wonderful and pleasing hit and miss effect.

3. Both pure and water-soluble wax crayons make stunning effects over acrylics and inks.

4. Splattering is probably the oldest trick in the book but still a really effective way to energize a dull area of the painting or simply to suggest sprays of water.

5. The jewel-like colours of artist quality soft pastel really lift a dull patch of colour if you drag the pastel over a textured area so that it catches all the peaks.

6. Using a sponge roller to apply paint leaves a very effective and random mark.

7. An oil pastel resist with two complementary colours makes striking combinations.

8. Scribbling with the pipettes of jars of ink creates wonderful and uneven lines.

9. Layering two different gouache colours and letting them dry, then rewetting random areas and scraping off the colour with a card, leaves these stunning abstract patches behind.

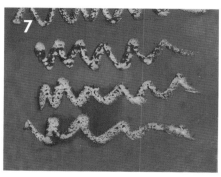

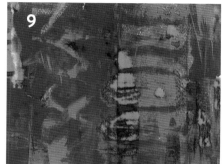

◁ **Woodland Study**
38 x 51 cm (15 x 20 in)
This quick and spontaneous study
of trees was done by dropping inks
directly over the watercolour paper and
dragging the ink with a card to shape
the trees. I painted the branches by
dipping the edge of the card into the
puddles of ink and just dabbing it to
suggest the branches and twigs. I used
a roller to apply lighter colour in
between the trees to get the effect of
light coming through. The splatters of
ink create some movement and energy
in the whole piece. I added some
brighter colours using blue, yellow and
bright orange oil pastels. The whole
image was done in minutes without
using brushes or stopping to assess
progress. This is another great exercise
for getting closer to painting in an
intuitive loose and free style.

The creative process

In painting, the creative process begins long before the brush touches the paper. Gathering ideas, turning them into usable source material, planning and composing your work, choosing your colours and preparing the surface are the preliminaries before you start to apply the pigments. Most important, however, is to recognize the creative potential of a subject and to turn the seemingly mundane into something extraordinary. This is a natural and instinctive process for gifted artists but with passion, hard work and dedication it can be nurtured and encouraged to flourish and develop.

◁ **Hampshire Yellow Fields**
37 x 40.5 cm (14 ½ x 16 in)

Sources of inspiration

'The real voyage of discovery consists not in seeking new lands but seeing with new eyes'
Marcel Proust

Inspiration is such an important aspect of the creative process, for it is the spark that motivates the artist to create in the first place. However, whether you are a composer, songwriter or painter, ideas don't just fall into your lap; they come to you through a process of hard graft. Inspiring ideas arrive at unpredictable moments and you need to be prepared to grab that moment. The traditional approach of carrying a very small sketch pad and a pencil is still the most reliable way of noting unexpected ideas as they arise, but it can be useful to collect back-up materials with your camera, smartphone, iPad or similar gadgets.

What inspires me to paint a landscape is usually colour, shape, pattern and texture. I am mainly motivated by how I can use layers to capture the essence of the landscape. I have no interest in depicting a recognizable landmark or subject and that is evident in the finished picture. Emotional involvement is the important factor here.

If you feel the urge to create art but are stuck for ideas, identify the elements that excite you artistically and you will never be short of inspiration. Is it colour, light, shadows, dramatic contrasts or landmarks that most excites you? Narrowing down all these options will help you to get a step closer to what inspires you to pick up your paint brush. This is not difficult today, with access to so many visually stimulating materials in galleries, in print and online.

Sources of inspiration don't have to be varied – indeed, some artists spend many years exploring a simple idea right on their doorstep in many different forms and continue to create unique and interesting art. Others spend a lifetime travelling far and wide to gather their source materials. However, a source of inspiration is not static – it is an evolving concept as you gain more experience along your artistic journey.

◁ Cornish Cottages by the Harbour
20 x 40.5 cm (8 x 16 in)
A quick harbour study made on a textured ground with gouache, watercolours and crayons.

◁ **In the South of France**
43 x 58.5 cm (17 x 23 in)
I used a combination of acrylic inks and watercolours for this quick sketch, leaving out a lot of unnecessary detail and focusing on the beautiful shapes of the buildings that had caught my attention. You can see that I let the drips run down and form the otherwise boring foreground.

Painting and sketching outdoors

Developing the skill of narrowing down the great outdoors to make a selective composition from a vast landscape is an important step in progressing as a landscape painter. Take advantage of any opportunity to go outdoors to paint or sketch; this may be an overwhelming idea at first, but with perseverance it will become a very rewarding experience. It helps you to interpret your back-up photographic material in a more meaningful and sympathetic manner in the comfort of your creative space at home. I take numerous photographs to record information such as the change of light and any details necessary to be able to continue fine tuning the painting back at the studio.

When painting en plein air, as it is known, it is often necessary to simplify your subject matter. Recognize the important aspects that excite you and leave out unwanted elements; you do not need to include an unattractively misshapen tree, a post or a gate just because they are there in the landscape. In other words, what you leave out is just as important as what you include. Making this distinction is an invaluable discipline that helps you to create artworks that have a clear statement to make, rather than confusing the viewer with too much irrelevant information.

Facing the challenges of painting outdoors, such as a limited range of materials, distracting sounds, ever-changing light and inquisitive passers-by, makes you into a more spontaneous painter and helps you to learn to improvise. It is also the best way of finding source material that is individual to you, allowing you to create unique artwork.

Composition

Space, line, shape, form, colour, value and texture are the elements of design that make up your painting. Rhythm and movement, discord and harmony, balance, variety and contrast are a few of the principles of design that help you to distribute these elements in the most aesthetically pleasing arrangement. Without the framework of a sound composition the painting can easily fall apart. There are some guidelines that can initially help you make the most dynamic composition, but in time, this will become an instinctive and selective process. Don't rush to break the following guidelines, though, until you are confident you are doing so effectively.

The rule of thirds is the traditional way of finding the ideal position for your focal point. Divide your paper into thirds vertically and horizontally and place your focal point on one of the four intersections. The focal point may be the biggest shape or group of shapes, the brightest light, the most vivid colour or the darkest tone – whatever will create the most impact and drama in your painting. Not every painting has a clear-cut focal point, but often the artist compensates with the use of colour, light or another compositional element to overcome this and avoid compromising the success of the painting.

Balance is created through the equal distribution of the elements, for example the proportion of lights and darks, busy and quiet areas, larger and smaller shapes and so on. It can be symmetrical or asymmetrical. In landscapes and seascapes it is important to avoid cutting the painting in half by placing the horizon line in the middle. Allocate a smaller area for the sky and bigger area for the foreground or vice versa.

Rhythm and movement is the repetition of elements such as shape, colour or texture in order to create an echo and movement within the painting.

Variety in the size, shape or colour of the repeated elements creates contrast and stops the image from becoming boring.

Emphasis and subordination directs the viewer's eye. Emphasis can be defined as the area that attracts the most attention – the focal point – while other elements play a supporting role to it.

Unity is created through an underlying common factor among the elements – for example an underpainting that shows through the top layers in small amounts and creates cohesion. You could say that it is the bass player in your painting orchestra and creates the beat that connects all the elements.

Simplification reduces the subject to the most significant elements in the painting and captures the viewer's attention without bombarding them with irrelevant information.

Structure is essential. Most representational images have a simple underlying structure that is largely hidden except to the artist's discerning and curious eye. The first task in composing is to abstract this simple design from the subject. Breaking down the real elements into simple geometric shapes helps you towards achieving this. Even the most complicated subjects can be reduced to their bare bones.

Nowadays, you have the advantage of being able to use various apps to achieve this, but I suggest that you get to grips with the task through the more traditional routes in order to become confident with tonal patterns and composing your painting.

Cropping and editing

Large paintings that are unsuccessful because they lack a cohesive composition can sometimes be a store of hidden gems. Before dispatching any of them to the graveyard of failed paintings, grab a few different mounts in various shapes and move them around the painting; you may be surprised to find some smaller images that work beautifully.

I often divide a big sheet of paper into various shapes with masking tape to take with me on outdoor painting days and use with just a limited palette. This is also useful when I am making sketches from photographic material I have gathered; it is so easy to focus on the important elements within a small area and make any necessary adjustments. The successful compositions can then be made into a bigger painting.

Lost and found edges

There are times when the style of a painting requires a clear and well-defined edge between the various shapes within the composition. In most Impressionist paintings, however, the play of lost and found edges creates ambiguity and encourages the viewer to interact with the painting. This is achieved by merging some of the edges into one another or the background, allowing the contour to disappear and then reintroducing it along another boundary. This leaves the viewer to use their imagination and explore the painting for much longer.

In watercolour painting you can achieve this by spraying the edges or simply wetting the area and letting one colour fuse into the other. In mixed media painting you have many tools such as soft or oil pastels, as well as various types of crayons and paints to soften and lose an edge. Aim for a good balance between crisp, well-defined edges and soft, diffuse contours. The linking of shapes within the painting through lost and found edges creates a closer relationship between the elements and makes not only an interesting and intriguing image but one that is more cohesive.

▽ Rainbow Woods
37 x 58.5 cm (14 ½ x 23 in)
This painting is a good example of the concept of lost and found edges. You can see how parts of the tree trunks merge into the background colour or the tree next to them and then reappear more defined further along. This treatment of the edges makes for more evocative images.

◁ **Tulips in the Woods**
38 x 56 cm (15 x 22 in)
This painting started with washes of colour, then the shapes of the tulip flowers and foliage were gradually carved out of the background washes by painting into the negative areas around them. This makes for a more balanced and cohesive composition.

Negative shapes

The concept of negative shapes in a painting is baffling for many novice artists. These are all the areas that are in between and around the shapes that constitute the subject matter. Balancing the negative and positive shapes within the subject is a necessary skill to master. This way the painting can progress while both the subject and the areas around it are dealt with simultaneously and sympathetically and the painting should stand a good chance of having a balanced and interesting composition.

Understandably, beginners are usually so preoccupied with all the positive components of their subject matter that they can be unaware of awkward negative shapes that they are creating. Conversely, for most experienced artists, addressing the negative areas often takes precedence over the positive shapes, as does the tone rather than the local colour of the objects. Luckily this concept will eventually become a natural and instinctive process as you gain experience. Here are a few pointers that should help you along the way.

• Divide the picture plane into areas of positive and negative shapes within the subject matter and make sure they provide variety, harmony and balance.

• Be aware of the areas where two adjacent shapes meet. If they look awkward, overlap the shapes to eliminate the unsightly negative shape.

• As you work out your negative and positive shapes, make sure that the subject fits comfortably within the picture plane. If you make the shapes too small the subject will become insignificant, while if they are too large you may not be able to get all the necessary elements of your subject within the space. Fitting the subject so that one or two elements go slightly out of the picture plane works well as it adds more weight to the subject and gives the viewer the idea that there is life beyond the confines of the painting.

The power of underpainting

There are times when preserving the white of the paper or any other support is crucial to the overall colour pattern of the painting, but if that is not the case, consider applying an underpainting first. There is more than one reason for doing this. Traditionally, in what is known as the indirect method of painting, a tonal pattern is created with the underpainting. In the absence of many colours it is easier to map out the light, dark and mid tones and create a structured tonal map to build the painting on. This is particularly useful if you are not confident about your handling of tone as it can help you to choose the right tonal values for each colour in your painting.

As the underpainting can affect the top layers, spend some time thinking through your choice of colour before the start of the painting. Choosing the complement of the dominant colour of your subject matter is an option. For example, a bright red can create a foil for a predominantly green colour scheme. This can add real sparkle and excitement as well as providing a unifying factor to the image if you allow tiny fragments of the red to show through in subsequent layers. Conversely, a more quiet underpainting allowed to show through can create respite from the more vibrant colours of the painting. So choose the mood you wish to convey by a complementary colour for vibrancy or an analogous colour (one adjacent to the dominant colour on the colour wheel) for a harmonious scheme.

For a sunny feel to your painting, choose a background of Naples Yellow, Raw Sienna or Yellow Ochre, or set an even brighter mood with a brilliant warm yellow or a cool lemon yellow.

◁ **Magenta Sky**
35.5 x 35.5 cm (14 x 14 in)
I chose Naphthol Red Light as an underpainting for this image. The orange-red makes the complementary green come alive and also works well against the blue of the sky as blue and orange are also complementary colours. The little dabs unify the image beautifully.

△ Hazy Light

51 x 51 cm (20 x 20 in)

Quinacridone/Nickel Azo Gold acrylic paint has given this painting exactly the warm feeling that the scene evoked in me at the time. I left the sky the same colour as it fitted the painting perfectly. The same yellow added to Dioxazine Purple created the velvety dark browns for the darker tones in the painting. Within the harmonious and limited colour palette, the small dabs of light green oil pastel and royal blue soft pastel stand out and add interest to the painting.

Demonstration 1:

Summer Meadow

In this demonstration I have chosen the warmest red-orange to counterbalance a predominantly cool carpet of wild blue and violet flowers in a summer meadow. The underpainting colour has a profound impact on the outcome of the painting.

Materials

Heavy body acrylic paints

Cadmium Red Light; Dioxazine Purple; Hansa Yellow Light; Phthalo Blue Green Shade; Quinacridone Magenta; Titanium White; Ultramarine Blue

Other materials

Oil pastels: Bright Turquoise; Turquoise Blue

Soft pastels: Light Blue Violet; Light Magenta

Wax crayon: Caran d'Ache Light Green

38 x 38 cm (15 x 15 in) mount board

25 mm (1 in) wash brush

△ **Stage 1**

Using the wash brush, I applied a rather uneven wash of diluted Cadmium Red Light over the whole board. The unevenness was deliberate, so that the small amounts of red that show through in the finished picture are varied in intensity. As an alternative, you could use watercolour, acrylic ink or gouache to apply the underpainting. I chose acrylic paint so that I could apply a thick brushstroke and thin it down by adding water to the brush and dragging it across the support.

Stage 2

I then made a dark-toned green with Phthalo Blue Green Shade, Hansa Yellow Light and a dash of Quinacridone Magenta to create the underlying structure of the composition. The dark lines form a path that will encourage the viewer's eye to meander through the painting.

Stage 3

I mixed a light blue-violet with Ultramarine Blue and Titanium White and applied it carefully over the sky area, allowing small fragments of the red underpainting to show through. With a cool Turquoise Blue oil pastel, I painted the distant fields. I then lightened the green mixture with more yellow and applied it unevenly across the field area to prepare the ground for the flowers to be painted over the top.

I added more colour to the trees and used the Turquoise Blue oil pastel to paint the background fields. I then strengthened the foreground dark colours further with Dioxazine Purple to create depth within the painting. At every stage the composition became clearer and stronger.

◁ In this detail of the finished painting you can clearly see that despite many layers and dabs of cooler colours, I maintained little fragments of red to unify and warm up the whole image. All the shapes become smaller as they recede from the foreground to give depth and perspective.

▽ **The finished painting: Summer Meadow 38 x 38 cm (15 x 15 in)**

To paint the flowers, I mixed a tint of Quinacridone Magenta and Ultramarine Blue and a light blue-violet from Ultramarine Blue and Titanium White. I added these in dabs over the dark framework of my composition to suggest the flowers. I painted further flowers with the Light Blue Violet and Light Magenta soft pastels to add texture to the meadow. You can see the foreground marks are larger; as they recede they diminish to create the illusion of depth. In between the pink and blue-violet flowers I used Turquoise Blue oil pastel and a vivid Light Green wax crayon for the stem of the foreground flowers. The small amount of red coming through not only unifies the painting but also adds a certain amount of warmth to a predominantly cool colour scheme. I blurred some of the divisional lines between the fields to create a lost and found effect, then added a touch of Bright Turquoise oil pastel to the sky to balance the colours further. Despite the fairly limited palette of colours the painting looks quite colourful.

Project 2:

Choosing the format of your painting

The orientation of your painting is the initial expression of your artistic statement and has a profound effect on the mood you wish to convey. The same subject can be framed in several ways, each one evoking a different feeling.

You don't have to conform to the familiar shapes of rectangular landscape or portrait formats; breaking out of the traditional ways of composing your painting can lead to exciting discoveries. Panoramic, square, or even circular and oval can all be effective. To get used to the idea of working this way, take a large sheet of paper and divide it into a few smaller, different shapes using masking tape. Pick a favourite subject and with a limited palette of colours use the various formats to make a range of compositions. This is a good exercise to get you used to different formats. Repeat the exercise with various subjects and decide on the best one for a larger piece of work.

When painting en plein air, try using viewfinders of different shapes, easily made by cutting apertures in cardboard, to capture the same scene in a variety of different formats.

Don't be a slave to the shape of your source material when painting from a sketch or photo reference – play around to find the most dynamic way of presenting your art work. However, do a few thumbnail sketches beforehand to avoid coming unstuck at a later stage.

▷ **Yellow Fields**
46 x 23 cm (18 x 9 in)
The image in this long, thin portrait format creates an impression of looking through a narrow window and provokes a feeling of anticipation that there is life beyond the confines of this tight visual field. Sometimes I paint in this format, while on other occasions I crop a section from a larger painting.

▷ Summer Fields
46 x 46 cm (18 x 18 in)

I find the division of shapes and forms of the same subject in a square format much more exciting. This format has become quite popular in recent years and gives a more dynamic and contemporary feel to the subject by enclosing the elements in a perfectly balanced area that encourages the viewer's eye to move in the more comfortable confines of a circle. The necessity for simplification within the square format helps to create more impact.

▷ Turquoise Sky
33 x 63.5 cm (13 x 25 in)

Horizontal formats are usually expansive and restful, giving a feeling of tranquillity as the eye moves gently from one side to another to absorb the information.

Beyond the surface: texture effects

As you gain more experience in painting in mixed media you will naturally begin to look beyond the superficial layer of your work. Multi-layering is at the core of working in mixed media, so your chosen support and ground preparation and how they affect the subsequent layers is central to the overall design and ultimately the final surface quality of your painting.

Texture is one of the fundamental elements of design and as such should be an integral part of the composition of your painting. In this chapter we shall be exploring a plethora of surfaces as well as primers, gels, pastes and mediums that can help you to create a feast of exciting visual and tactile textural effects in your painting.

◁ **Fields of Heather**
48.5 x 56 cm (19 x 22 in)

Choices of surface

Mixed media can be applied to numerous surfaces, from top-quality watercolour paper, acrylic paper, multimedia paper and canvas to panels of MDF primed with gesso and everything in between. Options such as acrylic glass (trade names include Plexiglas and Perspex), Yupo waterproof paper, aluminium and Ampersand panels can produce surprising and exciting results. However, whatever you choose, your support should be suitable for your very first layer of paint application.

For example, if you are starting with inks or watercolour an absorbent surface is more appropriate, unless you are choosing to apply washes on a semi- or non-porous primed support for some particular effect. If acrylic paints are to be the first layer your surface should have enough grip for them to adhere to the surface and not peel off at a later stage, so keep away from shiny or greasy surfaces. If you decide to paint on a smooth, hard surface such as a piece of glass, for example, you will need to buff the surface to create enough tooth. Paints and inks behave differently on each support, so the final surface quality of your painting depends on your choice of support and how you prime and prepare your ground. We shall be looking at a few different ways to prepare a ground in this chapter, plus a number of gels and pastes for some wonderful textural effects.

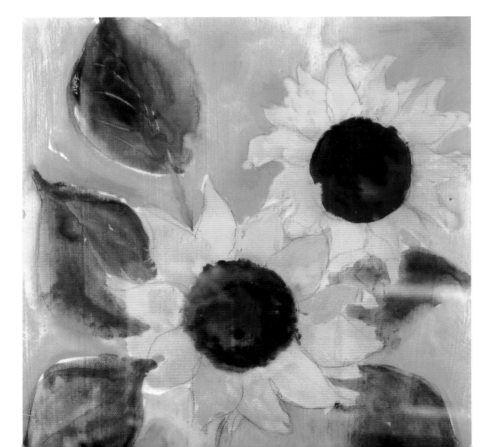

◁ Sheets of Plexiglas can be cut into various shapes and make a great alternative to other surfaces for acrylic, watercolour and mixed media painting. In this little exercise I applied a layer of fine pumice gel to create tooth and laid watercolour directly onto that. This required reverse painting, which means painting a mirror image of the subject so that it will look the right way round through the front of the Plexiglas.

△ This exercise shows the versatility of gesso. You can brush it on smoothly or roughly, scratch into it or sculpt it into any shape you want, perhaps leaving an imprint of a shape that you wish to come through the top layers of paint.

Texture effects with gesso

This basic primer, traditionally made from rabbit skin glue, chalk and white pigment but now most often acrylic, can do so much more than just creating a barrier between your paints and your chosen support, which is what it is primarily intended for. It can be applied smoothly or vigorously to show your brush marks through the subsequent layers; it can be scratched into or imprinted by various objects pressed onto it. Gesso should always be treated as a primer – do not mix it with your colours other than tinting it to prepare a ground.

The viscosity, smoothness or grittiness of gesso differs from one brand to another. You can buy white, black and clear gesso and some brands offer other colours too, although you can add colour to gesso yourself. For a very smooth finish try sandable gesso, available from Golden.

Gesso reduces the absorbency of your support a great deal and creates some fascinating visual effects with washes of acrylic inks. You can apply it all over or make it patchy to create a tension between the absorbent and non-absorbent areas of your painting.

Experimenting with other grounds

There are a number of alternative acrylic-based primers that can transform your support into an exciting surface for both wet and dry painting and drawing media such as pastels, graphite and pencils. With these, you will be able to customize your support to achieve a look and surface quality unique to your style.

Acrylic ground for pastels

Golden's range of grounds includes an acrylic-based primer that contains sand (silica) and creates tooth for both dry and wet media. Priming the support with this ground not only creates the perfect grip for a variety of dry media such as pastels and crayons but also a wonderful gritty surface for acrylic paints. This allows almost limitless applications for media that are typically confined to standard papers. The product comes in a thick consistency and is easier to apply if you dilute it 20–40 per cent with water. Apply it with a brush, roller or sponge to create a translucent and gritty layer on your support.

△ **Sketch of Poppy Field**
For this little sketch I used acrylic ground for pastels to turn a smooth card into a surface suitable for drawing media and pastel painting.

Absorbent and watercolour grounds

In general you cannot make a satisfactory watercolour or acrylic ink painting on a semi- or non-porous surface such as a gesso-primed canvas; some accept watercolour-type applications well enough, but many don't. By applying a layer or two of either watercolour ground or Golden absorbent ground you can prepare a paper-like absorbent surface, which can broaden the options on gesso-primed canvases. Golden absorbent ground can also be applied to a piece of card or a panel of wood to make it suitable for water media. It can be diluted by 25 per cent; to avoid the surface cracking, several thin layers are better than two thick coats. The surface creates some exciting visual effects that are different from those achieved on watercolour paper.

You can fix a watercolour painting on canvas by spraying it with watercolour fixative or a spray acrylic varnish to protect it from environmental damage. Nowadays you also have the option of canvases that are already primed for watercolour applications.

△ **Cornish Clifftop Flowers**
40.5 x 51 cm (16 x 20 in)
Two coats of Golden absorbent ground created a lovely surface similar to a smooth watercolour paper on the canvas. I usually let this layer dry fully before going in with washes of colour. Unless the pigment is super-staining, on this surface I can lift colour easily when I need to. Any mistakes can be rectified by using another layer of absorbent ground, which often leads to less tentative watercolours.

Acrylic gel mediums

One of the joys of working with a variety of wet and dry media is the ability to create tactile textures in your paintings. The most economical way of doing this is to take advantage of some of the acrylic gel mediums rather than using a large amount of expensive paint. These are in effect colourless paint as they are essentially made up of the same acrylic polymer but lack the pigment. Golden is one of the leading producers of these mediums and many of them are initially produced at the request of individual artists before they become widely available. A choice of soft, regular, heavy, extra heavy and high solid gels in gloss, matte and satin allows you to make really individual surfaces to paint on.

Gels can help you to build up textural layers prior to painting or they can be added to your paints to extend your colours further. You can also use them for priming your surface or glazing your painting. Some artists add natural sand and grit to create texture and volume in their paintings but these materials are not archival and may compromise the longevity of their paintings, whereas the artist quality gels are not only very effective but also long-lasting. They are resistant to chemicals, UV rays and water.

All acrylic products have an adhesive quality but the gels are especially good for the purpose of collage. Gloss gels and acrylic gloss mediums are perfect as they dry clear.

Using soft gel to extend paint

An economical way of using high-quality paints is to extend the colours by adding soft gel. You can use as much or as little gel as you wish to dilute the colour. The gel is white when wet but will dry to a clear finish, so it won't make a tint of your paint.

◁ You can see here how a small blob of colour can be extended with gel for reasons of economy. The gel dries clear, so that the colours retain their tone.

Building texture with regular gel

Regular gel is heavier than soft gel and has the exact consistency of the heavy body paints. It is great for adding to these paints to volumize them for impasto applications or for making a textured ground prior to painting.

△ **Field of Irises**
40.5 x 40.5 cm (16 x 16 in)

Once my underpainting of Naples Yellow dried, I painted the sky with a mixture of Phthalo Blue and Titanium White. I used light green to suggest the foliage of the irises, and a mixture of Dioxazine Purple, magenta and white for the flower heads. A mix of Dioxazine Purple and Cadmium Yellow provided all the dark tones within the field and for the mass of trees. Using a palette knife and mixing the paints with copious amounts of regular gel give the painting its impasto style and spontaneous and lively appearance.

Heavy and extra heavy gels

Acrylic paint has a tendency to lose at least 30 per cent of its volume as it dries after application. To paint in an impasto style you may need to use a lot of paint, making it quite an expensive exercise. Heavy, extra heavy and high solid gels are all thicker than heavy body acrylic paints and provide a more economical way of making highly textured paintings. The gels can be added to the paint or applied to the support and sculpted into the desired textures prior to painting. They are all available in gloss, semi-gloss and matte, so you can choose the particular finish you feel would enhance your painting.

△ **Turbulent Sea 1**
21.5 x 28 cm (8 ½ x 11 in)
In this painting I used heavy gel gloss with the more runny Golden Fluid colours, so the painting has a lovely glossy and shiny finish. The gel has helped to retain some brush marks which normally level out when using just the Fluid colours.

▷ **Turbulent Sea 2**
21.5 x 28 cm (8 ½ x 11 in)

For this painting I chose extra heavy gel matte and heavy body paints and the whole painting process was quite different. This combination offers a greater degree of control and the perfect viscosity to retain expressive brush marks. I personally favour the matte finish for my style of painting.

◁ **Rocks**

These rocks were sculpted with a palette knife and extra heavy gel gloss. You can manipulate the gel to achieve your desired shapes. Once the gel dried I then painted over the rocks with inks and Fluid colours. The inks tend to run off the gloss gel and separate into lovely colours. I love the way the darker tones pool in the grooves and create the necessary darker values. It is also easy to lift colour that is over the gloss gel to create highlights.

Clear tar gel

It took a while for me to become comfortable with this funky gel and start having fun. Golden clear tar gel has a long rheology, which means that it can drip from your palette knife in a long, stretchy and stringy fashion and create a maze of beautiful patterns on your support. You can use it to suggest particular textures, such as ropes in a marine painting, or apply it in an abstract manner to merely add interest to the painting. You can use the gel clear as it comes or add a drop or two of Fluid or High Flow colours.

Clear tar gel and the gels described above level out as you pour them onto a non-absorbent support, such as a plastic sheet, so they make an ideal choice for making beautiful acrylic skins for collage.

◁ **Long Grass in the Hedgerow**
25.5 x 48.5 cm (10 x 19 in)
In this painting I used clear tar gel to suggest the long grasses in the foreground. I like the way the gel resists washes of colour and shows through.

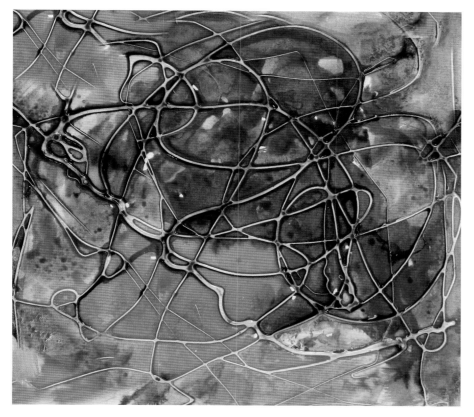

◁ Here clear tar gel is used as a resist. I dripped the gel on a piece of mount board and created some random patterns, then applied a wash of High Flow acrylic ink in blue and magenta. As you can see, the gel resists the washes and creates boundaries. When transparent colours are used the patterns resemble a stained glass window.

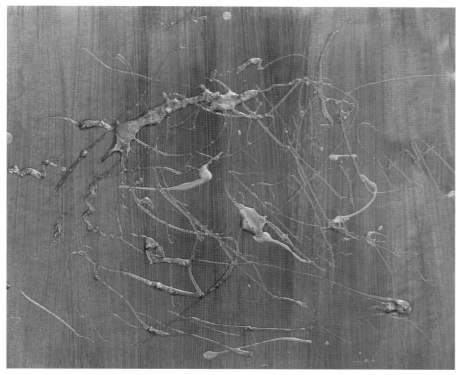

◁ I added a few drops of Iridescent Bright Gold Fluid acrylic to the clear tar gel and dripped it over a Manganese Blue background. Be careful with the amount and consistency of the colour you add so that the gel doesn't become too heavy and lose its pouring ability. As an example, in two tablespoons of clear tar gel I only put two small drops of Fluid or three to four drops of High Flow colours.

Gels with aggregates

I remember experimenting with all kinds of natural materials and glue to create a rough texture in my paintings, but apart from it being rather messy a concern about longevity was always at the back of my mind. Nowadays there are gels with added aggregates to help you emulate certain textures in your subject matter. Glass bead gel, clear granular gel and pumice gel are just a few of these incredible, versatile and archival gels. The gels don't have one specific function and manifest themselves in different ways in the hands of different artists.

Pumice gels

The fine grade of pumice gel has, as you might expect, very finely ground pumice. This gel dries to a slightly greyish tone and has a fine gritty surface that is ideal for drawing media but also works well with water media, especially inks, because of its absorbent quality. The gel can also be mixed with paint and applied to a surface. I often use this gel to create tooth for soft and oil pastels. Used as a primer, it creates a wonderful ground for acrylic painting too. I sometimes mix it with Open acrylics to give a more gritty body to the slightly creamy paints.

Coarse pumice gel has slightly larger grains of pumice and works well for suggesting any rough texture you may wish to emphasize in your landscape, while the extra coarse grade has much larger pieces and is ideal for suggesting rough pebbled ground or similar textures. These grades both create highly absorbent surfaces; I love the way the washes of ink sink into the gels. Rubbing a soft pastel over the extra coarse pumice gel also creates some lovely hit and miss colour effects.

▷ This detail from Pebble Beach shows how the whole painting is done over pumice gel, with fine pumice gel at the top and then coarse and extra coarse pumice gel in the foreground. The highly absorbent nature of pumice gel soaks up the ink washes beautifully and yet allows the colours to shine.

△ **Pebble Beach**

51 x 40.5 cm (20 x 16 in)

This kind of beach scene is the ideal subject for pumice gel. I have used all three grades to create recession.
I usually apply the gels and dry the surface before going back with the washes of colour. Pumice gel is quite
absorbent and the washes sink beautifully into the gel.

Glass bead gel

Golden glass bead gel actually does contain glass beads and dries to a clear luminous and shiny surface. You can use your imagination as to where you can incorporate this rather attractive gel to enhance your painting. Overpainting it with transparent High Flow, Iridescent and Interference colours can produce some amazing results. Alternatively, you can scrape glass bead gel over a light colour to create a wonderful shimmering effect.

Clear granular gel

This gel has a similar look to extra coarse pumice gel except that the acrylic granular solids dry to a translucent finish so the gel doesn't alter the colour you mix with it. This is one of my favourite gels, especially for floral paintings where the centres of the flowers can be enhanced with translucent texture.

▷ **Echinacea Field**
21 x 28 in (54 x 71 cm)
The round balls of polymer and glass make both granular and glass bead gels a perfect choice for the centre of certain flowers. Here I have used the clear granular gel for the flowers in the foreground and the glass bead gel, which has smaller balls, for the flowers further away. You can use both gels for many other applications or experiment with other flowers such as daisies or sunflowers.

Acrylic pastes

Most gels are either transparent or translucent, so when I need opaque texture I tend to use Golden pastes instead as they contain either marble dust or other fillers that give them absorbency and an off-white or greyish tone. Their surface allows the washes to sink in and create enchanting passages in the painting. Each type has its own unique properties that you can explore to discover where it can create the textures or grounds that might enhance your painting.

Moulding pastes

There are a number of moulding pastes (the same as modelling paste) that can either create a rough texture over a smooth surface or conversely smooth out a rough surface by filling in the grooves. These take the versatility of mixed media to another level with so many different options.

In the Rocky Beach painting (right) I have used a variety of moulding pastes to shape and sculpt the rocks. The washes of colour run over the less absorbent pastes and sink into the absorbent ones, creating quite an abstract pattern that can easily be read as a jumble of rocks.

△ **Regular moulding paste** dries to a hard yet flexible opaque film. It blends with colours to tint and extend paint and also works really well as a ground for acrylic paints.

△ **Extra heavy gel/moulding paste**, a blend of a gel and a paste, dries to a satin, semi-opaque finish. I love this paste for using with stencils to create raised passages in paintings.

△ **Light moulding paste** is a lovely white, fluffy, lightweight paste that is useful for building thick absorbent texture on really large pieces of work without making the painting too heavy. Matte, opaque and absorbent, it gives a totally different surface quality to any other gel or paste.

◁ Rocky Beach
46 x 51 cm
(18 x 20 in)

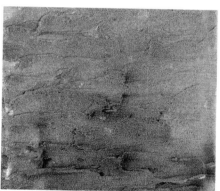

△ **Hard moulding paste** If you need a really tough and durable texture that you can even drill patterns into, hard moulding paste is great as it dries to an extremely hard opaque film. You can hand carve it or use a power tool.

△ **Coarse moulding paste** creates a rough surface with a similar tooth to sandpaper and remains translucent up to 2mm (1/8 in) thickness. Used as a primer, it creates a wonderful ground for all types of wet and dry media; mixed with Fluid or heavy body acrylics, it creates a dense paint that retains peaks and brush strokes.

Fibre paste

I use this paste a lot in my cityscapes and harbour scenes, where I feel that it can represent the rough texture of urban buildings or cottage walls, and when I need an area in the painting to resemble a rough watercolour paper. You can apply this paste in any thickness you wish; for a thinner, smoother finish, skim it with a wet palette knife or trowel.

To make a fibre paste skin, apply the paste over a plastic sheet and peel it off once it is dried. You can then either paint on it just like a piece of rough handmade paper or tear it up to use as collage in a larger painting.

◁ Shown here is fibre paste on paper with washes of colour, giving the characteristic rough-textured effect.

◁ **Cornish Cottages**
38 x 48.5 cm
(15 x 19 in)
Fibre paste is ideal for suggesting the rough rustic walls of these Cornish cottages. Simply apply the paste with a palette knife and let it dry before adding washes of colour.

◁ **African Landscape**
51 x 40.5 cm (20 x 16 in)

I applied crackle paste over my canvas using a trowel, making the middle sections thicker for the largest crackle and laying thinner applications towards the horizon and at the sides of the painting. The next day I was delighted to be rewarded with exactly what I had in mind. I then applied simple washes of High Flow Phthalo Blue, Red Iron Oxide and Quinacridone/Nickel Azo Gold over the whole canvas. I painted the trees with heavy body paint, using the same colours mixed together to make my darkest greens. I felt the end result was quite effective with a very limited palette of colours. The whole painting is about the parched foreground, suggested most effectively with my crackle paste.

Crackle paste

This quite light and fluffy white paste is opaque and absorbent. It is visually very similar to light moulding paste. The crackling texture makes it one of the most enjoyable pastes to experiment with, but unfortunately it is also the most temperamental. You need to be patient, as the crackles do not appear immediately and sometimes you need to leave the paste overnight to cure and crackle. The best way to apply it is by a palette knife or trowel on a rigid surface, such as heavy paper, card or stretched canvas. Thinner layers create smaller shapes, so for larger crackles apply the paste thicker.

Crackle paste can give you many different options for imaginative representational or abstract textures. Once the crackles appear you can choose to apply a wash of colour over the whole area or paint each section individually for a mosaic effect.

Project 3: Creativity with stamps and stencils

Using gels with stamps and stencils is another exciting avenue to explore for making wholly abstract pieces or abstracted backgrounds for contemporary representational paintings. Stamps and stencils help you to make precise, regular shapes as opposed to the more organic look of the marks made freehand with a brush or other tools. A combination of stencils and more loose and free paint applications is another appealing feature of mixed media painting.

There are numerous ready-made shapes available in both stamps and stencils, or you can make your own to represent the particular shapes you want in your painting. To make simple stencils, take a sheet of cartridge paper and apply a layer of acrylic medium (matte or gloss) or soft gel on both sides to seal and strengthen the paper. Once it is dried, draw the shapes that you wish to transfer to your support. Cut around the shapes with a craft knife and your stencil is ready to use. Of course, there are special gadgets that can do these jobs for you in double quick time!

◁ This experiment is based on a piece by Patti Brady, a well-known American abstract artist with brilliant and innovative ideas. I applied washes of Magenta and Phthalo Blue watercolour on a piece of card first, then squeezed soft gel gloss through a set of tree stencils. I lifted the watercolour washes from the areas that were not protected by the gel medium. The result is fantastic. I think these are great little pieces by themselves but they can also be incorporated into larger pieces of work or into backgrounds. You can try this using various shapes of stencils to create intriguing areas in your paintings.

▷ △ I have a large collection of stamps, including swirls and flowers, that I incorporate in some paintings to make the backgrounds more interesting.

Squeezing gels through stencils will make wonderful raised patterns that can create really interesting passages in your paintings. Alternatively, you can make an imprint of stamps on the heavier gels and pastes. An easy way to make a stamp is to cut a shape from a piece of foam board (for example a leaf shape) and stick it to a block of wood for an easier grip. Dip the foam board into an ink pad and then make an imprint on your paper, just as you would with a ready-made but quite expensive stamp. Common materials such as bubble wrap, coins and sequin relief are examples of simple objects that can be used just like a stamp, pressed direct into the gel to leave an imprint. Here are a few examples for you to try in this project.

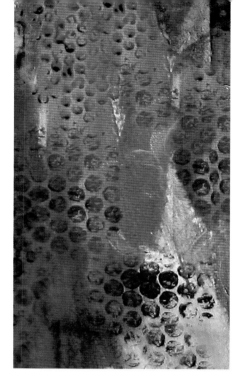

△ This basic sequin stencil has helped me so many times as a filler in backgrounds where I need some kind of ordered shape to create interest. Sometimes I just put the colour through and other times I make it raised by laying some heavy gel as well as colour.

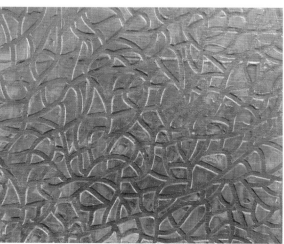

◁◁ Here I mixed heavy gel semi-gloss with Iridescent Gold and squeezed the gel through an abstract stencil. This pattern makes a great background for various subjects.

◁ **Block stamp sample**
This is one of my favourite stamps, dipped in bright gold heavy body acrylic and printed on a paper primed with black gesso to enhance the gold paint.

Collage

Incorporating collage in your mixed media artwork adds yet another dimension to it, contributing interesting and seemingly random textures and colours. Paintings can be predominantly made up of collage materials, such as pieces of text, exotic handmade papers and found objects, or the collage can be used merely to suggest a particular texture.

While collage can be applied in a complex and elaborate manner, it can be very simple and yet very effective. In this chapter we shall be exploring a few creative ways with collage to enhance a mixed media painting.

◁ **Polperro**
48.5 x 63.5 cm (19 x 25 in)

Collage materials

The kind of materials used for collage always depends on the artist's personal approach. However, the most common items are tissue paper, exotic Indian handmade paper or Japanese rice paper, found objects and pieces of text cut from books, magazines or newspapers. Materials such as scrim, cheesecloth, netting from fruit packaging and similar items can all create quite interesting passages in the painting.

Working with collage is perhaps one of the best ways to lose your inhibitions and bring out your inner child. I use it quite moderately in my work as I like the interaction of washes of colour on the surface of the paper with the collaged parts. I feel that this creates a more exciting and chaotic surface that I can then manipulate to whatever shapes I need in my painting.

▽ **Boat Race**
48.5 x 63.5 cm (19 x 25 in)
In this fun piece all the sails and bodies of the boats are made up of pieces of handmade paper, magazine cuttings and tissue paper. The colours are reinforced with inks to protect them from fading. I applied the collage pieces first before adding washes of inks followed by heavy body acrylics to paint the sea.

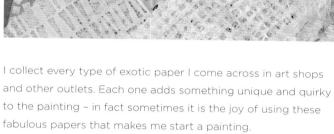

I collect every type of exotic paper I come across in art shops and other outlets. Each one adds something unique and quirky to the painting – in fact sometimes it is the joy of using these fabulous papers that makes me start a painting.

Here I used a roller to colour my tissue paper with diluted Manganese Blue and Cobalt Teal heavy body acrylics. When it dried I applied a thick layer of gold mica flakes to add a real sparkle to the otherwise quite ordinary coloured tissue paper.

For this piece of customized tissue paper I applied a layer of gel on a double layer of the paper and allowed it to form its natural creases. When it dried I applied Fluid and heavy body colours in pink, red and bright aqua green. Finally I added gold and bronze on top. This makes a very beautiful and exotic-looking paper.

It is great fun to make your own handpainted collage pieces. I like to use white tissue or good-quality cartridge paper as a base and then add my colours by roller, drips, drizzles, drawing and spraying. These unique pieces are great to add to the paper or canvas as the starting point for an abstract or semi-representational painting.

How to apply collage

Just as the choice of collage pieces varies from one artist to another, so does their application. Your collage items can be torn to give an organic look or cut up in geometric shapes, depending on your subject. All acrylic products act as glue, so any of the acrylic mediums or gels can be used successfully to adhere your collage pieces. Gloss medium is perfect as it dries completely clear and doesn't affect the colour, but PVA glue is a more economical and perfectly suitable alternative.

The process of your painting can start with sticking down the collage pieces prior to applying washes of colour. Conversely, you can begin with washes of colour and apply the collage as and when you feel a certain colour or texture can enhance the painting. You should always reinforce the colour of collage pieces such as coloured tissue paper, handmade paper and even magazine cuttings with lightfast inks as their colourant is usually a natural dye, which will eventually fade. However, the existing colour of the collage gets you to your desired colour a lot quicker.

One of the key things to note is that collage can be absolutely magical when it is in the right place but quite hideous when it is not. Unfortunately when this happens the collage commands a lot of attention, though not in a good way. Fortunately there are ways and means of eliminating the eyesore by pulling it off or covering it with paint, gesso, a more suitable piece of collage or a texture medium. However, there are times when the painting begins to have a terribly laboured look and there is no other rescue measure to be had. With experience you will get better at choosing and applying collage to avoid this issue.

◁ **Layered Landscape**
40.5 x 51 cm (16 x 20 in)
The visual impact of this painting is the result of the interaction of the ink washes with the tissue and a variety of hand-made papers.

Iridescent colours

◁ A selection of Iridescent and Interference colours. The shimmering effect of these colours has a mesmerizing quality.

Golden Iridescent are a stunning family of colours that can jazz up your painting beautifully. These colours are synthetically produced to have the same kind of reflective quality as the wings of dragonflies and some butterflies. They are all derived from mica platelets, though Iridescent Pearl has an extremely thin layer of Titanium White and, based on the reflection and refraction of light, produces a fabulous pearlescent effect. Iridescent Gold, Copper and Bronze have an iron oxide coating that creates their particular hue, plus a pearlescent effect. As they respond to the effect of light, the more light that shines on them the more they show their amazing brilliance. Gloss gel and varnish enhance their iridescent quality while matte gel dampens it down. Other examples of these colours are Silver, Micaceous Iron Oxide, Stainless Steel and Gold Mica Flakes, each with their own unique hue and shimmering effect. They really shine when applied on dark surfaces and add a real sparkle to the painting.

△ **Colourful Pebbles**
33 x 48.5 cm (13 x 19 in)
A rough layer of light moulding paste overlaid with collage tissue paper on hot pressed paper provided the perfect textured ground for drips and drizzles of High Flow and Fluid colours. Once the blues and purples dried, I went on to add dabs of Iridescent Gold and Bronze to give the piece that extra punch. The combination of colours with gold and bronze makes for a stunning image.

▽ The Golden Sky
46 x 46 cm (18 x 18 in)

This painting was done over a ground textured with gesso and coarse pumice gel. I applied strips of handmade paper in the middle section. The dark tone of Anthraquinone Blue and Phthalo Turquoise Fluid acrylics created the perfect dark backdrop for the Iridescent Gold and Bronze to show their rich and opulent hues. The brushed-on gold in the sky creates a lovely sunny atmosphere.

Interference colours

Golden Interference paints are a series of stunning colours made from mica platelets with a thin and transparent coating of titanium dioxide. The effect of these colours is through reflection, refraction and interference of light. Experiment by applying them on a light surface and what you will see is a very pale hue; as you move the piece of paper you will also see the complement of the colour, so they flip back and forth between their true colour and its complement. They truly come to life when you apply them over a dark surface or by adding black to the colour.

Mixing them with other acrylic colours can create some beautiful results, since their shimmering quality makes the colours much more interesting. It is rather difficult to appreciate their beauty in photographs, but you can really see their effectiveness when you come close to a painting.

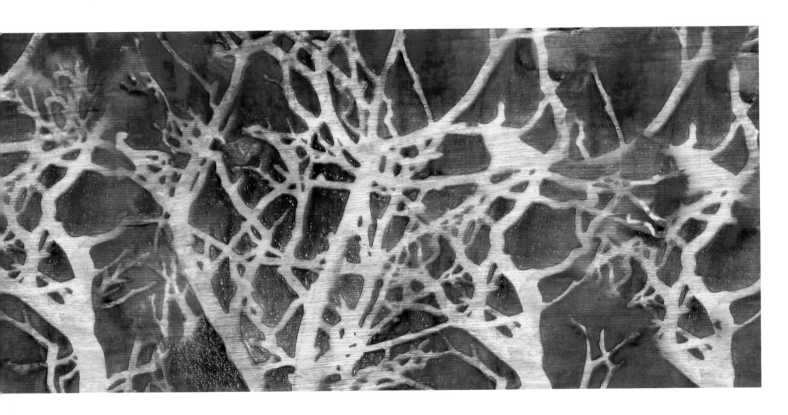

△ Skeletal Trees
20 x 25.5 cm (8 x 10 in)
Here I applied a layer of soft gel gloss to a card and let it dry before laying a coat of black gouache on the surface. I used a stencil to squeeze another layer of soft gel on top of the card, then washed out the black gouache as well as I could, which left all the areas of the tree stencil almost white. I then painted the surface with Interference Blue and Violet. The true colour of the stencils only shows up where the colour goes over the top of black.

▽ Harbour by Night
46 x 46 cm (18 x 18in)

For this experiment I combined Fluid Violet, Blue and Green Interference colours with clear tar gel and dripped them in rope-like shapes over a foundation of heavy body Manganese Blue, Anthraquinone Blue and Violet. I then painted the simplified harbourside cottages with the same Interference colours over a dark blue background painted with Anthraquinone Blue heavy body acrylics. I used dabs of gold to suggest the lit windows of the cottages. Cut-up pieces of bookbinding material seemed the perfect collage material to describe the lobster pots.

Getting creative with unusual colours

Some of these unusual colours combine well with primary colours and create mesmerizing effects. Some behave in a unique way, such as the Iridescent Bronze shown here. Micaceous Iron Oxide dries to a glittering and sandpaper-like finish, so it makes a wonderful ground for any drawing medium. There is great fun to be had with these alternative colours, so do give them a try.

▷ For this abstract piece I sprayed the paper with water and dropped in Phthalo Blue Fluid colour in various saturation strengths. While the paper was wet I also dropped in Iridescent Gold fine Fluid colour, which blended in nicely with the blue in some places. I then applied more heavy body gold over the top to create a flowing pattern, taking care not to make it too dense. I love the soft and floating shapes that have been created. The combination of the gold and the blue create a rich and striking effect.

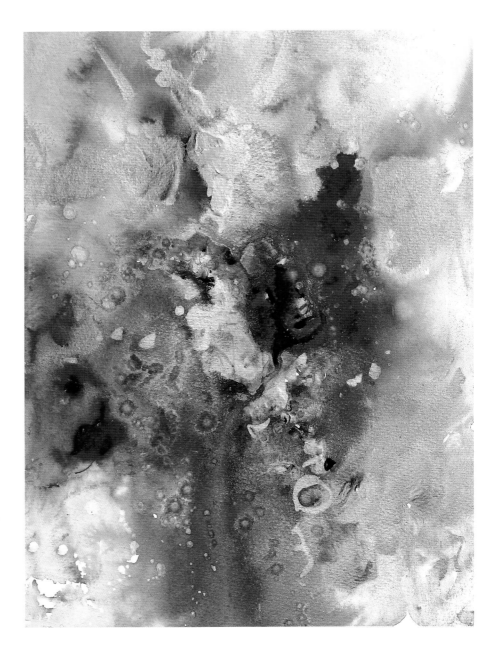

◁ This is a sample of Iridescent Bronze, which separates into a beautiful aqua green when used in washes of colour. Here I applied a wash over a foundation of transparent glass bead gel and opaque and absorbent light moulding paste. The two different levels of absorbency can provide interesting surface quality.

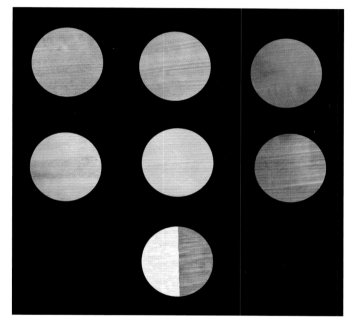

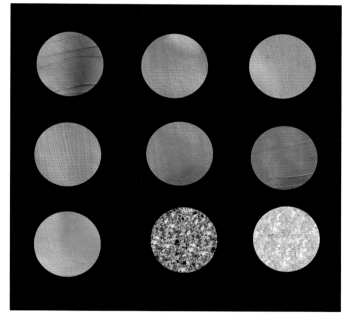

△ **A few samples of Interference colours (left to right)**

Interference Gold, Interference Green, Interference Blue, Interference Red, Interference Orange, Interference Violet

The last circle is painted half white and half black. You can see the true colour of Interference Violet on the black side but on the other side you can just discern a light violet. Though it doesn't reproduce well in print, if you move the paper, holding it close to you, the colour flips back and forth between violet and its complement, yellow.

△ **A few samples of the Iridescent colours (left to right)**

Iridescent Stainless Steel, Iridescent Bright Gold, Iridescent Silver (Fine), Iridescent Gold (Coarse), Iridescent Copper (Fine), Iridescent Gold Deep, Iridescent Pearl. Gold Mica Flakes, Pearl Mica Flakes

Demonstration 2:

Caribbean beach

This demonstration takes a simple subject and, through the use of collage and texture materials, makes it more interesting. It is really about transforming the surface of your painting to add a tactile quality.

Materials
Saunders High White hot pressed
    425 gsm (200lb) paper
Unison Orange soft pastel

Acrylic inks
Phthalo blue; Process Cyan;
Raw Sienna; Red Earth; Titanium
White

Heavy body acrylics
Buff Titanium; Cobalt Tea; Light
Ultramarine Blue; Naples Yellow;
Phthalo Blue; Pyrrole Orange;
Titanium White; Ultramarine Blue

Collage materials
Acrylic gloss medium
Cotton fibres
Fruit netting
Tissue paper, dark blue, light blue
    and green

Texture products
Fine, coarse and extra coarse
    pumice gel

△ **Stage 1**
I used acrylic gloss medium to apply strips of tissue to the paper in the sea area. Working downwards, I applied fine, coarse and then extra coarse pumice gel to create the necessary recession. The larger bits of pumice suggest pebbles. I used the cotton fibre and fruit netting to suggest an abandoned part of fishing net.

△ Stage 2

I wetted the sky area slightly with water and flooded a wash of Process Cyan at the top, letting it graduate to the horizon line, then used Phthalo Blue at the horizon line to paint the sea. I returned to Process Cyan and then Teal as I got closer to the shoreline. I added a wash of Raw Sienna to the beach, overlaid with a wash of Red Earth ink, then applied a diluted wash of Red Earth to the sky to balance the colours.

▷ Stage 3

Once the first layer of ink dried I started to build up the layers in the sea with heavy body acrylics, at the same time integrating the collage pieces into the painting so that they suggest the darker tone of the water. I used layers of Ultramarine Blue, Phthalo Blue, Light Ultramarine Blue and Cobalt Teal to suggest the ebb and flow of the water. I added layers of Naples Yellow and Buff Titanium to the sandy part of the beach.

▷▷ The finished painting: Caribbean Beach 61 x 48.5 cm (24 x 19 in)

I applied a mixture of Phthalo Blue and Red Earth inks in the foreground to give some weight to the bottom part of the beach, then created a grey by adding Titanium White ink to the same mixture and dragged the colour over the netting and that part of the beach around the net. Once that layer dried I added a layer of Cobalt Teal to the netting, which highlighted it amid all the texture in the foreground. I dragged a stick of Orange soft pastel over the texture of extra coarse pumice gel to highlight some of the pebbles, then splattered Pyrrole Orange paint to add more colour in the front. I highlighted the edge of the waves with Titanium White, stood back from the painting and felt that it had reached the finished stage.

▷ This detail of the foreground textures in the finished painting shows how the collage and texture products help to create a tactile surface with plenty of interest.

Colour through the seasons

The transformation of nature through the passage of one season to another presents a refreshing change to the palette of the landscape painter and for many artists it is one of their greatest sources of inspiration. Though the transition is gradual and seamless with many overlapping features, each season conjures up specific colours in our mind's eye. In this chapter we shall explore a selection of the most prominent colours in spring, summer, autumn and winter.

◁ **The Four Seasons**
51 x 71 cm (20 x 28 in)

△ I Dream in Colour
35.5 x 35.5 cm (14 x 14 in)

Choosing your colours

Colour is perhaps one of the most powerful aspects of your composition, since the mood and atmosphere of your painting is directly affected by your choice of colour scheme. A basic understanding of colour mixing, tonal values, colour temperature and the role of complementary colours and pigment properties is fundamental to the success of your painting. My suggested basic palettes below should help you to narrow down your palette to a few pigments with which you can mix a wide range of colours from vibrant to muted, plus all your dark values and neutrals.

It is important to get to know the properties of your pigments so that when you buy single-pigment primary colours you do so for a reason; for example, having two warm yellows because one is transparent, such as Indian Yellow Hue, plus an opaque one such as Cadmium Yellow Deep because you need the covering power. Also, when you buy ready-made colours (blends) it should be because you need consistency and convenience, not because you cannot mix the same colour with your basic palette. In dry media such as soft and oil pastels you can buy introduction sets to give you a base selection of colours and thereafter add favourite colours in single stick form.

In each season we shall be exploring useful mixes, plus some additional colours that you can add to your art box for convenience.

Basic palette: modern colours

Anthraquinone Blue; Phthalo Blue Green Shade; Naphthol Red Light; Quinacridone Magenta; Hansa Yellow Medium; Hansa Yellow Light (Lemon Yellow); Phthalo Green, also a single-pigment colour and a great addition to these primaries as a useful base for mixing greens; Titanium White and Zinc White. This palette consists mostly of synthetic organic modern pigments that are highly lightfast, transparent, intense colours and produce mixtures with superb clarity.

Basic palette: classic colours

You can also choose from the more traditional classic colours that offer slightly more subdued and natural mixtures, such as Ultramarine Blue, Prussian Blue Hue, Cadmium Yellow Light, Alizarin Crimson Hue and Cadmium Yellow Deep or Indian Yellow Hue plus Titanium White, Burnt Sienna, Yellow Ochre and Viridian Hue.

These inorganic pigments are generally of lower chroma and some are opaque, so they generally produce colours that are closer to those in nature. I often mix different colours from both palettes to suit my project at the time.

Spring

The arrival of spring heralds the start of new beginnings, the season of the rebirth of nature. As nature rejuvenates, so does the palette of the landscape painter. Spring presents a fusion of fresh, vivid and yet delicately subtle colours to explore. Multi-coloured crocuses scattered across the fresh green grass, sunny yellow daffodils and forsythia, purple hyacinths and irises, orchards in bloom and the magical carpet of bluebells in the April woods all offer endless inspiration for the discerning artist.

▷ **The Edge of the Forest**
47 x 47 cm (18 ½ x 18 ½ in)

Fresh and subtle spring colour palette

The colours of spring are fresh, soft and subtle, so I tend to mix a lot of tints or diluted watercolours and acrylic inks. The chart below lists a small selection of useful colours for spring landscapes and flowers. Some of these can be bought in ready-made tubes for convenience and consistency but I find the inconsistency of my own colour mixes is part of the charm of a painterly and Impressionist style of painting.

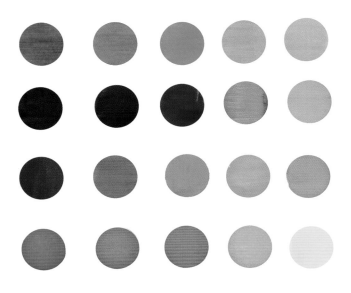

◁ **1st row, left to right:** Phthalo Green as a base colour with Hansa Yellow Light or Lemon Yellow creates vibrant greens. Adding more yellow takes you through mid and lime green until just a touch of green into the yellow creates a beautiful vivid yellow-green. Adding Titanium White makes a lovely light tint.

2nd row: A touch of Quinacridone Magenta is added to tone down and darken Phthalo Green for warmer, more natural spring greens. The final swatch is a warm and beautiful tint.

3rd row: Phthalo Blue is added to Phthalo Green to make even cooler distant greens.

4th row: Light blue-violet is achieved by mixing Ultramarine Blue and Titanium White plus a dab of Quinacridone Magenta; Ultramarine Blue with more Quinacridone Magenta and Titanium White mixes a warmer violet; Quinacridone Magenta and Titanium White produce a soft pink for cherry blossoms, crocus and pink primroses; Cadmium Red Light or Naphthal Red Light plus Cadmium Yellow Deep Hue or Hansa Yellow Deep plus Titanium White mixes a beautiful soft peach for spring flowers such as primroses; Hansa Yellow Light plus a touch of Titanium White gives the colour for daffodils and yellow crocuses.

▽ **Dancing Tulips**
16.5 x 40.5 cm (6 ½ x 16 in)
In this painting, I used Fluid Green Gold and acrylic inks Flame Orange (Daler-Rowney FW) and High Flow Phthalo Blue, then used the pipette of my Payne's Grey (Daler-Rowney FW) ink bottle to outline the tulips and their foliage. The orange-red tulips make a striking complementary combination with the blue background.

△ **Pink Cherry Blossoms**
19 x 40.5 cm (7 ½ x 16 in)

In this painting I used a split complementary colour scheme of magenta opposite blue-green and yellow-green (the two colours either side of green, the complementary of red). When combined, these colours create a wonderful buzz and energy in the painting. I used heavy body acrylics on a ground of coarse moulding paste applied in a patchy manner. The canopies of the trees were painted with lots of splattering in light and dark magenta. I chose magenta as my dominant colour and allocated most of the green area to the light green with only accents of blue-green to break the monotony.

Striking combinations

Complementary colours – orange and blue, red and green, yellow and violet – make striking combinations placed next to each other and their vibrancy is enhanced. Yellow and blue are also regarded as a particularly pleasing combination, employed a great deal in the textile industry to create stunning fabrics. The Impressionists used this concept of adjacent complementary colours to maximum effect in their magnificent paintings full of sublime light and colour. You can darken a colour by adding a small touch of its complement. If you increase the ratio of the mix the two colours finally neutralize one another and make brown, grey or near black.

1. Complementary colours of Magenta and Cobalt Teal create a buzz when placed next to each other.

2. The combination of a reddish orange and blue creates maximum vibrancy in both colours.

▽ **A Touch of Spring**
46 x 46 cm (18 x 18 in)

In April, yellow fields of rapeseed bring sunshine to the British countryside. I really love the soft and gentle predominantly analogous colour scheme of these early spring fields. The transition of yellow-greens through greens to blue-greens and blues is really easy on the eye. However, the primary combination of yellow and blue helps the colour scheme to avoid becoming boring. The painting was done with heavy body colours and soft and oil pastels on a Not surface Saunders Waterford watercolour paper. I made the splattering of colours in the foreground with a mixture of Golden High Flow, Hansa Yellow Light and Titanium White.

△ **Sunlit Woodland**

46 x 43 cm (18 x 17 in)

This painting started with small square dabs of oil pastel on my paper and washes of Lemon Yellow and Indian Yellow acrylic inks. I then used High Flow Dioxazine Purple to create the tree trunks. The whole image is about my response to encountering the drama created by the contrast of the very light new spring foliage against the dark backlit tree trunks.

Field of Crocuses: the painting process

In this painting I wanted to exaggerate the excitement of encountering the multi-coloured crocuses scattered over a carpet of fresh springtime grass. I created a slightly textured ground on my Not surface watercolour paper by applying a patchy, random layer of regular gel matte and some tissue paper collage in selected areas.

I then applied washes of High Flow Quinacridone Magenta and Phthalo Blue and Daler-Rowney FW Light Green acrylic inks over the textured ground. Once I had my base colour in place, I started adding heavy body paint with a palette knife, which covered some of the washes of ink while allowing snippets of bright colours to shine through and suggest the flower heads. I also used dabs of water-mixable wax crayon and oil and soft pastels to enhance the colours, highlight an area or create a new flower head. The sky was largely painted using a palette knife with strands of Fluid colour flicked across to bring interest and a lively atmosphere into the painting. Titanium White was used throughout to make tints of light purple and magenta as well as suggesting the white crocuses. The process of this painting was quite organic and summed up my personal response to the scene.

◁ **Field of Crocuses**
56 x 76 cm (22 x 30 in)

Summer

The intermittent rain and sunshine of the British summer provide an explosion of colour in the countryside as well as in gardens. Wildflower meadows, hedgerows, fields of poppies, daisies, lavender and sunflowers create a profusion of colours. The vibrant hues of early and mid-summer and the deeper, richer greens with the golden hedgerows and fields of late August give you ample opportunity to indulge in your love of rich, saturated colours as well as offering plenty of shapes, patterns and textures to explore.

▷ **Hampshire summer meadow**
56 x 76 cm (22 x 30 in)

Summer colour combinations

1 The combination of Cadmium Red Light and Light Green (ready-mixed) is stunning and full of impact.

2 The contrast of Cobalt Blue and the same Light Green is more restful as they are neighbours on the colour wheel.

3 The combination of Cerulean Blue and Teal is even more tranquil as the colours are quite close on the colour wheel.

4 In comparison, Teal looks as though it is vibrating against the orange-red.

◁ **Woodland Corner**
20 x 40.5 cm (8 x 16 in)
The greens become deeper and richer as we go through the summer months. I made a variety of different greens for this painting, using Phthalo Green as a base colour, then added accents of pastels over the acrylic base to bring lighter tones.

▷ **Hogweed Patterns**
16.5 x 40.5 cm (6 ½ x 16 in)
Hogweeds swaying in the breeze make walking or driving along country lanes a joy in the summer months. In this painting I used coarse pumice gel to emphasize the texture of the flower heads. I established the background with washes of Yellow Ochre ink and used a combination of Dioxazine Purple and Yellow Ochre to create the dark tone within the hedgerow. I added the stems and other greenery using sticks of soft pastels in Apple Green and dabs of Turquoise Blue oil pastel.

Glorious hues of the summer colour palette

Colour is one of the most powerful aspects of your painting. It is the first element that draws the attention of your viewer, so it needs careful consideration to ensure the overall success of your painting. With so many brilliant colours to choose from in the summer months it is important to harness your excitement in choosing your colour scheme. Too many vibrant and saturated colours together can easily create visual noise rather than a memorable and pleasing visual experience. Don't forget to include darks and neutrals to make the more brilliant colours shine.

The greens become deeper than those of the spring and the colour of summer flowers are generally bolder and brighter.

▷ **1st row, left to right:** Prussian Blue and Hansa Yellow Medium make a series of warm and natural greens from very dark to the beautiful tint of light warm green.

2nd row: Ultramarine Blue and Cadmium Yellow Deep Hue mix a great olive green. The colour at the end of the row has added blue and Titanium White for distant greens.

3rd row: Pure Quinacridone Magenta in its glorious bold undertone; Quinacridone Magenta and Ultramarine Blue; Phthalo Blue and Titanium White for seascape and summer skies; Phthalo Blue in its beautiful undertone; Quinacridone Magenta darkened with a touch of Phthalo Green for deep aubergine darks.

4th row: Quinacridone Magenta with a touch of Titanium White for a medium magenta; Cadmium Red Light Hue for poppies and other orange-red flowers; Cadmium Red Light Hue and Cadmium Yellow Deep Hue mix a bright and fabulous orange; Hansa Yellow Deep; Phthalo Green with a dab of Quinacridone Magenta for clean near-blacks.

◁ **Sunflower Fields, Provence**
40.5 x 40.5 cm (16 x 16 in)

I used complementary violet and blue to give vibrancy to the yellow in this painting of sunflower fields. The painting was done on a piece of mount board primed with gesso, which makes an excellent ground for acrylics. I then painted the whole composition with heavy body colours mixed with some matte heavy gel to create more body for the paints. All the browns are a mix of Dioxazine Purple and the warm Hansa Yellow Medium and Deep. The limited colour palette is broken by a few accents of a very light brilliant blue oil pastel, which brings another complement to the yellow and adds interest.

▽ **Detail of Sunflower Fields 2**

This detail of another sunflower field painting shows the difference when the same subject was painted over a ground of coarse pumice gel, giving a totally different look and feel to the surface quality of the painting.

▽ **Contrast of yellow orange and violet blue**

Yellow and blue are visual complementary colours and the combination is used to maximum effect right across the design industry and in painting.

Cornish Clifftop: the painting process

In this kind of painting, gels can be used to maximum effect as they emulate the texture of the rocks beautifully. I used a variety of gels, such as heavy and extra heavy gel matte, to sculpt the rock shapes with a palette knife. In a few places I stuck some crumpled tissue paper collage onto the gel as well to create even more texture. I used a large household brush to gesso the foreground to let the brush marks come through the subsequent layers and add interest. When the washes of ink go over a prepared ground such as this the colours tend to find their own way and seem to pool in the grooves, creating wonderful light and dark patterns that can be read as the form of the rocks. I used a card and heavy body paint to bring in the foreground grasses and plants and splattered Titanium White ink to suggest the water spray. By using a roller to apply the highlights on the cliffs at the back I emphasized the texture on the rocks. This kind of approach helps to bring a spontaneous look to the painting and the process is both unpredictable and exciting.

◁ **Cornish Clifftop**
43 x 63.5 cm (17 x 25 in)

Autumn

As the summer draws to a close, the atmospheric light and the glowing autumn colours go a long way to compensate for the arrival of the cooler weather. This season presents us with the most seductive of all the colour palettes and proof that mother nature is the greatest colourist of all. With the golden hues against the deeper blue of a clear autumn sky, the profusion of red berries and the multi-coloured leaves on the forest floor, there is much to explore in the ephemeral beauty of this magical season.

▷ **Autumn Woods**
48 x 63.5 cm (19 x 25 in)

The autumn palette

Autumn offers the landscape painter the opportunity to play with an array of fabulous golden hues of yellow, amber and saffron and deeper reds, russet and scarlet. It is a rich and wonderful palette of colours. Complementary colours of violet, blue and deeper greens bring in the striking cool contrasts against the warmer hues. Here are some of the colours that can be added to your art box and some that you can mix.

◁ **1st row, left to right:** Indian Yellow Hue is a transparent golden yellow; Quinacridone/Nickel Azo gold is transparent orange; Quinacridone Burnt Orange is deeper gold and a beautiful rich colour; Quinacridone Crimson is a deep cool red with undertones of orange; Pyrrole Orange is bright and vivid.

2nd row: Hansa Yellow Light, Hansa Yellow Medium and Hansa Yellow Deep; Raw Sienna, a beautiful earth yellow; Cadmium Orange made from Cadmium Red Hue and Cadmium Yellow Deep.

3rd row: Burnt Sienna; Burnt Umber; Dioxazine Purple in its undertone; Dioxazine Purple and Indian Yellow Hue; Yellow Ochre, similar to Raw Sienna but a bit more dense.

4th row: Cobalt Blue for a deep blue autumn sky; olive green mixed from Ultramarine Blue and Cadmium Yellow Deep Hue; tint of olive green; velvet brown made with Dioxazine Purple and a touch of Burnt Sienna; Quinacridone Magenta in its glorious undertone is the colour that appears on the leaves of Virginia creeper and some acers.

△ **Golden Reflections**

41 x 19 cm (16 x 7 ½ in)

The stunningly rich saffron colour of Indian Yellow Hue acrylic ink was the perfect choice for this lakeside autumn landscape. I then flooded washes of Carbazole Violet and Quinacridone Red watercolour to suggest the shrubs and the reflections. Once they were dry, I added rich dark browns made with Dioxazine Purple and Indian Yellow heavy body colours to deepen the colour of the lakeside shrubs. Then I applied heavy body Lemon Yellow to bring the light golden reflections onto the water. Small dabs of soft pastel in cooler violets and blues bring a necessary contrast to the predominantly warm colour scheme of the painting.

◁ **Chinese Lanterns**

16.5 x 40.5 cm (6 ½ x 16 in)

These extraordinary flowers never cease to amaze and delight me in the same measure and I never get tired of painting them every autumn. I used washes of acrylic inks Daler-Rowney FW Flame Orange, Light Green and Purple Lake and High Flow Phthalo Blue on a piece of mount board to create random shapes that could be turned into flower and foliage shapes at a later stage. Most of the painting was then done through painting into the negative spaces and bringing the shape of the flowers to appear from the chaos of colour washes. I used secondary colour triads of green, purple and orange with little dabs of blue to contrast against the orange.

▽ The complementary colours of yellow and violet placed next to one another create a fantastic energy in a painting. You can make either colour the more dominant to change the balance of the colour scheme.

1 Yellow orange and pink violet.

2 Lemon yellow and blue violet.

▽ **Autumn Gold**

46 x 46 cm (18 x 18 in)

This painting is built up of many layers, starting with the cool earthy yellow of Raw Sienna, followed by cool Cadmium Yellow Pale for the distant hills. The complementary violets work beautifully against the variety of yellows and the orange hues. The silhouetted trees were painted with Dioxazine Purple mixed with Cadmium Orange and bring in the much-needed verticals against all the horizontal shapes of the fields. The painting was done over a textured ground with gesso, which made the application of Lemon Yellow oil pastels a bit hit and miss. I used some gold mica flakes in the foreground to add a touch of sparkle.

△ **Autumn Leaves**
43 x 33 cm (17 x 13 in)

I look forward to finding the wonderful and random still life set-ups of fallen autumn leaves; they make a wonderful exercise for getting to grips with painting the negative shapes. For this exercise I flooded the paper with all my favourite autumn colours – Fluid Quinacridone Burnt Orange, Magenta and Nickel Azo Gold – and let the colours mingle, then went into the negative space behind each leaf to cut it out from the background while making another shape behind to avoid outlining or making halos. I used a mix of Daler-Rowney FW Purple Lake and Phthalo Blue to create lovely rich velvety browns with Quinacridone Burnt Orange in the negative spaces to create depth. The lighter and brighter colours come forward and the darker ones recede, giving a three-dimensional effect to the painting.

Tangled Autumn Hedgerow: the painting process

I chose a Not surface Saunders Waterford watercolour paper for this painting as I like its texture coming through the paint layers. I prepared the ground with patches of gesso and heavy gel matte, leaving most of the paper free to react with the paints. A wash of Flame Orange acrylic ink over the whole paper created a lovely warm background, while a mix of Phthalo Blue and Burnt Sienna provided the darks to create depth within the hedgerow. I then used heavy body Hansa Yellow Light, Medium and Dark, Cadmium Orange and Burnt Sienna to describe the mass of hedgerow plants over the dark areas. Light violet blue pastel on the distant hills created a striking contrast against the complementary bright orange of the sky. Sequin relief used as a stencil was the perfect option to suggest the roughness of the stone wall behind the hedgerow plants.

◁ **Tangled Autumn Hedgerow**
46 x 60 cm (18 x 23 ½ in)

Winter

Far from the cold, colourless and bleak image it often conjures up in the mind's eye, in reality the winter landscape takes on a quiet and elegant kind of beauty. Winter months bring a respite from the riot of colours and instead offer the landscape painter the opportunity to enjoy the most sophisticated palette of beautiful warm and cool greys. Skeletal trees and hedgerow plants, snow-covered hills sparkling in the gentle light of the winter sun and the ethereal beauty of hoar frost are just a few examples of the store of inspiring subjects to explore and enjoy in the winter months.

▷ **Winter Landscape**
40.5 x 46 cm (16 x 18 in)

The greys of the winter palette

The winter palette is all about colourful greys, those understated and elegant hues that are so easy on the eye, tranquil and beautiful. A splash of colour such as a red coat stands out brightly in a winter landscape because there is no competition among the surrounding neutrals.

My chosen palette for winter consists of blues, magenta, violet and in contrast to those colours, Naples yellow, yellow ochre, orange red, teal and turquoise. If you mix two complementary colours, exactly opposite each other on the colour wheel, in equal amounts, they neutralize each other and make grey or brown. Most of the time we mix near-complementary colours and the resulting greys are biased towards a colour. To achieve a range of beautiful greys, mix the complementary colours and vary the proportion, then add white. These are beautiful hues to work with and the winter palette gives you the chance to fully enjoy their gentle beauty.

◁ **1st row, left to right:** The classic mix of Ultramarine Blue and Burnt Sienna yields a beautiful near black or dark brown. I added Yellow Ochre and mixed it with white for a very light yellow grey. I added a little more of the yellow to achieve a lovely earth yellow.

2nd row: I mixed Phthalo Blue and Cadmium Red Light, to make a lively black, then added more blue plus white; then a little more red to make it neutral grey; then more blue and then more white for a couple of lovely blue greys.

3rd row: First is a greyed-down purple made with Ultramarine Blue and Quinacridone Crimson plus a little white. I added more white for a soft violet grey; more white plus a little more crimson for a soft pink grey; then more blue; and more white for a blue-violet grey.

4th row: Cobalt Teal makes a great contrast in winter scenes against grey; then a grey yellow from a mix of Raw Sienna and a touch of purple; Naples Yellow is perfect for the gentle yellow colour of the winter sun; a greyed-down green with Phthalo Blue, Magenta and Hansa Yellow Light plus a little white; finally, a great neutral grey that is a mix of Ultramarine Blue and Burnt Sienna in equal proportions with white.

Grey with other colours

 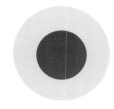  

Notice how the same grey appears quite light when it is placed against a dark brown background but much darker against the light yellow background.

A neutral grey background intensifies brighter hues beautifully. However, notice how it vibrates against the red but the contrast is rather more restful against the light blue.

◁ **Snowdrop Parade**
15 x 61 cm (6 x 24 in)

I used an analogous colour scheme for this painting of the snowdrops. Yellow greens, pure green, blue greens, teal and violet blues are all gentle neighbouring colours that create a tranquil backdrop for the white flower heads. White flowers give you the opportunity to play with the effect of light. I used heavy body acrylics and touches of oil pastel for the highlights in this painting.

△ **December Afternoon Snowfall**
16.5 x 40.5 cm (6 ½ x 16 in)

This late afternoon scene is about the soft and gentle shadows that the trees cast over the snow-covered ground. Most of the snow is described with light blue violet and cool greys; the white is only just visible in a few spots hit by the late afternoon light. The painting was done on a gesso-primed board using mostly heavy body acrylic paints, though there are touches of bright oil pastels in teal and violet blue.

▽ Winter Trees
30.5 x 30.5 cm (12 x 12 in)

Skeletal trees stand proud like magnificent sculptures in the winter landscape and are just as beautiful as when they are shrouded in a canopy of green foliage. In this painting, I started with a chaos of warm and cool yellows and greens as a background, then enjoyed playing with purples and blues over it, allowing the background colour to show through in a few areas. I applied a royal blue soft pastel to lift the distant trees.

△ **Remains of the Snow**

40 x 40 cm (15 ½ x 15 ½ in)

I used collage and texture gel like paint to build up the textured areas of the mountains and the foreground. Strands of tar gel created interesting linear marks. I like the contrast of the cool turquoise of the collage paper against the warmer purple overlay and accents of fiery orange complement the blue background. Scraping white and the pale violet over the foreground helped the textures to come to life, and paper collage gives the mountains a three-dimensional feel that is hard to achieve with just paint.

Snowstorm: the painting process

Snowflakes swirling in the haze of colourful Christmas market lights was the inspiration behind this painting. I flooded High Flow Ultramarine Blue and Quinacridone Magenta acrylic inks over the watercolour paper and moved the paper around to let the inks mingle. In the process they made a series of soft and hard edges. I then drew the trees using mostly the pipette from my ink bottles and acrylic marker pens. Once the layers dried fully, the fun began. I made a few puddles of Titanium White and Quinacridone Magenta, Titanium White on its own and Ultramarine and Titanium White inks and splattered the surface with these colours to create the snowfall effect. The result summed up the magical atmosphere of that night.

◁ **Snowstorm**
47 x 63.5 cm (18 ½ x 25 in)

▷ Colourful coastline
41 x 58.5 cm (16 x 23 in)

Acknowledgments

My sincere thanks and gratitude to the following as without their support this book would not exist.

Cathy Gosling for commissioning the book and believing in me, the help and support of Jocelyn Norbury and Nicola Newman at Pavilion Books. Diana Vowles for the very thoughtful and sympathetic editing, it was great working with you again.

Mark and Barbara Golden for being the most amazing visionaries, Patti Brady, the director of the Golden Working Artists' Program, for the ocean of ideas you share with us and being the coolest artist on the planet, and Pat Pirrone at Golden Artist colours for being the oasis of calm we all turn to for help and advice. Catherine Frood at St Cuthbert's Mill, Jason and Sandy Mackie at Global Art Supplies, I am so grateful for your continued support and amazing products which are a joy to work with. Last but not least, a huge thank you to all my wonderful students and supporters for appreciating the way I see the world.

Index

References to illustrations are in *italic*.